Barry Mills
Marvin R. Shanken
Rodney D. Strong
Robin Kelley O'Connor
James Trezise
Mike Stephens
Louis P. Martini

windows
ON THE WORLD

COMPLETE
WINE COURSE

Kevin Zraly

STERLING PUBLISHING CO., INC. NEW YORK

acknowledgments

I would like to express my appreciation to M. Shanken Communications, Inc., of New York City—publishers of *Impact* wine and spirits newsletter; *Market Watch* magazine; and *The Wine Spectator*—for supplying information used in this book.

I am indebted to the winemakers and grape growers throughout the world who contributed their expertise and enthusiasm for this project. The signatures on the end papers represent some of the people whose help was invaluable to me.

designed by Jim Anderson
earlier editions by Stephen Topping, Felicia Sherbert &
   Robert Hernandez
this revision edited by Keith L. Schiffman

10 9 8 7 6 5 4 3 2
© 1995 BY INHILCO, INC.
REVISED EDITION PUBLISHED BY STERLING PUBLISHING COMPANY, INC.
387 PARK AVENUE SOUTH, NEW YORK, N.Y. 10016
DISTRIBUTED IN CANADA BY STERLING PUBLISHING
C/O CANADIAN MANDA GROUP, ONE ATLANTIC AVENUE, SUITE 105
TORONTO, ONTARIO, CANADA M6K 3E7
DISTRIBUTED IN GREAT BRITAIN AND EUROPE BY CASSELL, PLC
WELLINGTON HOUSE, 125 STRAND, LONDON WC2R 0BB, ENGLAND
DISTRIBUTED IN AUSTRALIA BY CAPRICORN LINK (AUSTRALIA) PTY LTD.
P.O. BOX 6651, BAULKHAM HILLS, BUSINESS CENTRE, NSW 2153, AUSTRALIA
MANUFACTURED IN THE UNITED STATES OF AMERICA
ALL RIGHTS RESERVED

LIBRARY OF CONGRESS CATALOG CARD NO.: 84–26851
STERLING ISBN 0-8069-8493-7

CONTENTS

dedication

First and foremost, to my parents, Charles and Kathleen, and to my sisters, Sharon and Kathy, who have been a constant source of encouragement and understanding throughout my life.

To John Novi, for allowing me to learn about wines at the Depuy Canal House in High Falls, New York.

To Craig Claiborne, for giving the Depuy Canal House a four-star rating, which helped the restaurant's wine list grow to include 125 selections.

To Father Sam Matarazzo, who inspired me to take my study of wine to Europe.

To Peter Bienstock, who shared his older vintages with me.

To Herb Schutte, who gave me my first job in the wine business.

To Ron Koster and to Ulster County Community College, for allowing me to teach my first wine course.

To Vincent Barcos, from whom I first heard about Windows on the World.

To Joe Baum, creator of Windows on the World, who had the original concept of hiring a young American as cellarmaster.

To Alan Lewis, first director of Windows on the World, who hired me and was instrumental in the wine program.

To Toni Aigner, former president of Inhilco, who was the initial force behind this book.

To Mohonk Mountain House in New Paltz, New York, where ideas come easy.

To Raymond Wellington, for his editorial contributions and for writing the section about wine in restaurants.

To Kathleen Talbert, whose concepts helped greatly in the writing of this book.

To Burton Hobson, president of Sterling Publishing Co., Inc., who had the faith to put "another wine book" on the market.

To Felicia Sherbert, my editor, without whom this book could not have been written.

To Sara Hutton for her contributions to my later editions.

To Rebecca Chapa, who manned a lonely outpost in the World Trade Center.

To Stephen Topping, contributing editor for the first edition, who rejoined me ten years later to edit a revised edition.

To Andrea Immer, a wizard at everything, whose research and editorial contributions to the 1995 revision were essential.

And most of all to my wife Ana and our new vintages Anthony and Nicolas.

foreword

I remember vividly my first glass of fine wine. It was more than 25 years ago, and I recall that from that point on, all I wanted to do was learn all I could about wine.

Back in those days, you started with French wines, then moved on to Italian, Spanish or German wines; there was little talk of California wines. I went both to bookstores and libraries in search of books that could increase my knowledge. The books I found were often encyclopedic in nature—500-page volumes that made the topic of wine seem overwhelming.

Before I knew it, my interest in wine had developed into a passion, until finally it became my profession. Working in a restaurant, I came to realize that diners didn't need to know everything there is to know about wine, but I also discovered that most of them did want to learn more than they already knew.

The solution seemed simple to me: Someone had to write an introductory guide. As time went on, I was fortunate to meet some of the authors of the great wine books I had read. I asked some of these authors if they'd consider writing a simpler guide to wine, but they usually responded that there was no need for such a book.

I had never intended to write a book, but I became convinced that someone had to fill the need—my wine students kept asking me to give them something easier to read. And so it began. *Windows on the World Complete Wine Course* is one of my greatest accomplishments. I would have been happy just to sell one book; to help demystify wine for just one person. Instead, to date we have sold more than 500,000 copies of this book.

I would like to thank all of my colleagues in this business—the restaurant owners, hoteliers, retailers, wholesalers, importers, educators, and hospitality management schools—who have recommended this book as "the simple guide to wine."

We have updated this book at least nine times since it was first published. But in the ever-changing world of wine, ten years is an eternity, so I took a fresh look at the book, from start to finish, to change what needed changing, and to leave in place the information that's still valuable. I suppose many authors, faced with the opportunity to revise, would try to add to a book, but I've learned that "less is more." So I've tried to make the book even simpler and, thereby, I hope, clearer.

Not that the wine world is any less dynamic than it was ten years ago. Here is just a taste of the decade's developments:

- A broad shift in California-wine consumption—from generics to varietals; ten years ago who would have thought a Gallo Chardonnay would sell for $30 and a Gallo Cabernet Sauvignon for $60?

- The reunification of Germany, adding two new wine regions in eastern Germany

- Publicity about the so-called "French Paradox," and the role of moderate wine consumption in a healthy lifestyle

- The great decade of the 1980s in Bordeaux—with the red wines getting even better, and the white wines making great quality strides

- Quality enhancement continuing in the wine regions of Spain and Italy, as vintners learn to combine old-style traditions and new-style technology. (Speaking of Italy, who'd have thought ten years ago that the Italians would market a $60 Chardonnay?)

- The global re-emergence of the wines of Chile, Argentina, and South Africa; the broad popularity of Australian wines

- World-class wines from Long Island, New York

- Increased use by European wineries of the American-style practice of varietal labelling

Of course, as is always the case with wine, there's much more. But enjoying wine should be easy. I hope you enjoy my "simple" guide to wine.

I welcome all comments and suggestions, and would be happy to answer any wine questions you might have.

Write to:
    Kevin Zraly
    Windows on the World
    One World Trade Center
    (106th floor)
    New York, NY 10048

iNTRoduCTioN

I first heard about Kevin from one of my European associates. Kevin had come to visit our winery during his self-training in Europe. He decided that the only way to learn about wine was to visit the wine country. For eight months he toured the vineyards of France, Italy, Germany, Spain, and Switzerland. Somehow he made an impression—in blue jeans, on a very small budget, but with the right questions and a passion to learn. Europeans encourage wandering students—they can tell the real student from the phony one. They know that Americans have an insatiable thirst for knowledge.

Kevin's interest in wine started during his student days in New Paltz, New York. He took a job as a part-time waiter at the Depuy Canal House in nearby High Falls, and ended up as the manager of the only four-star restaurant in the Catskills. Since his job included the ordering of wine, he decided to learn more on the subject.

He returned to New York City, knowing a lot about wine, and was hired by a wine-and-liquor wholesaler to sell accounts that were more interested in Wild Irish Rose than in Meursault and Château Lafite. Before you knew it, he was the wine buyer and sommelier at Windows on the World, which ultimately turned out to be the largest wine account in America, possibly in the whole world. The job title was cellarmaster, and he continued to expand the responsibilities of the position. He created what is probably the most innovative and most frequently revised wine list in the world. After all, with knowledge and a word processor and computer there is no longer any need to carve a wine list in stone. He trained a staff second-to-none to suggest and serve the wine, and, inevitably, he started a wine school. That wine school, being in the financial center of New York, has taught more top executives than any other how to select and enjoy wine.

The reward for success in America is promotion. Kevin was named Wine Director in 1980, the same year he started the wine school. Besides teaching the wine classes, he started entirely new ventures along with *The Wine Spectator:* The California Wine Experience and the New York Wine Experience, each a three-day spectacular, where 1,000 people from across the country listen to lectures, attend tastings, seminars, and happenings, and meet the people who make wine. To see Kevin supervise the mechanics of a tasting that has 1,000 people sample a dozen wines is to witness a person who could hold his own as the stage manager of the Metropolitan Opera. The task involves 12,000 glasses, and all 1,000 people are served twelve wines at precisely the same time without mix-up. And wonder upon wonder, he has trained others to organize such happenings as well as he does.

It was inevitable that Kevin would write a wine book sooner or later—and that it would be different from any other wine book. It is not written to impress the world with Kevin's knowledge or insight, both of which he has enough of and to spare. It was written to be less rather than more. It is reminiscent of that old saying: "If I had more time, I would have written a shorter book." Well, Kevin has written a shorter book. He has written the essential wine book, a succinct guide to the essentials—a basic guide that does not weigh you down with unnecessary information or erudition, which would only hamper you in your journey through the labyrinth of wine. And yet this no-nonsense guide is not lacking in the necessary trivia to make the material entertaining as well as informative—those little hooks of extraneous facts which are so essential for the mind to remember facts. The information is presented in a well-designed format, it is easy to use as a guide or reference book, and yet it is interesting enough to read at one sitting. Small wonder, then, that his publisher tells me that, since its initial publication a decade ago, Kevin's book has been the best-selling hardcover book on wine.

In addition, the section on how to create a wine list and stock a wine cellar in a restaurant is the best account I have ever read on the subject. It is both diverse and economical, and it will no doubt serve as a blueprint for many a wine list across the land. The section titled "Wine in Restaurants," written by Raymond Wellington (former director of wine services at Windows on the World), is a delightfully informative look at the ritual of ordering wine.

This book represented one of the first of a number of innovative, education ventures by Kevin in the world of wines. He gains new ideas for "spreading the wine faith" in his extensive contacts with the neophyte and the connoisseur. There exists an enormous amount of information about wine, which most other writers seem to complicate. This early venture has gained Kevin an enthusiastic new following among wine lovers and new wine drinkers.

—Peter M. F. Sichel

prelude to wine

You're in a wine shop looking for that "special" wine to serve at a dinner party. Before you walked in, you had at least an idea of what you wanted, but now, as you scan the shelves, you're overwhelmed. "There are so many wines," you think to yourself, " . . . and so many prices." You take a deep breath, boldly pick up a bottle that looks impressive, and buy it. Then you hope that your guests will like your selection.

Does this sound a little farfetched? For some of you, yes. The truth is that this is a very common occurrence for the wine beginner, and even for the intermediate, but it doesn't have to be that way. Wine should be an enjoyable experience. By the time you finish this book, you'll be able to buy with confidence from a retailer, or even look in the eyes of a wine steward and ask with no hesitation for the selection of your choice. But first let's start with the basics—the foundation of your wine knowledge. Read carefully, because you'll find this section invaluable as you relate it to the chapters that follow. You may even want to refer back to this section occasionally to reinforce what you learn.

For the purpose of this book, wine is the fermented juice of grapes.

What's fermentation?

Fermentation is the process by which the grape juice turns into wine. The simple formula for fermentation is:

Sugar + Yeast = Alcohol + Carbon Dioxide (CO_2)

Sugar is present naturally in the ripe grape. Yeast also occurs naturally, as the white bloom on the grape skin. However, this natural yeast is not always used in today's winemaking. Instead, laboratory strains of pure yeast have been isolated, each strain contributing something unique to the style of wine. The fermentation process ends when all the sugar has been converted into alcohol, or the alcohol level has reached around 15 percent, which kills off the yeast. The carbon dioxide dissipates into the air, except in the case of Champagne and other sparkling wines, where this gas is retained through a special process.

Why do the world's fine wines come only from certain areas?

A combination of factors are at work. The areas with a reputation for fine wines have the right soil and favorable weather conditions, of course. But, in addition, these areas look at winemaking as an important part of their history and culture.

Is all wine made from the same kind of grape?

The major wine grapes come from the species *Vitis vinifera*. In fact, both European and American winemakers use the Vitis vinifera, which includes many different varieties of grapes—both red and white. However, there are other grapes used for winemaking. The native grape variety in America is the species *Vitis labrusca*, which is grown widely in New York State. *Hybrids*, crosses between *Vitis vinifera* and *Vitis labrusca*, are planted primarily on the East Coast of the United States.

The following are the three major categories of grapes and a sampling of the varieties found in each one:

VITIS VINIFERA	VITIS LABRUSCA	HYBRIDS
Cabernet Sauvignon	Concord	Baco Noir
Chardonnay	Catawba	Seyval Blanc

What are the three major types of wine?

Table Wine: approximately 8 percent to 14 percent alcohol
Sparkling Wine: approximately 8 percent to 14 percent alcohol + CO_2
Fortified Wine: 17 percent to 22 percent alcohol

All wine fits into at least one of these categories.

Winemaking begins in the vineyard, growing the grapes. This is crucial to the whole process.

Where are the best locations to plant grapes?

Grapes are agricultural products that require specific growing conditions. Just as you wouldn't try to grow oranges in New York State, you wouldn't try to grow grapes at the North Pole. There are limitations on where vines can be grown. Some of these limitations are: the growing season, the number of days of sunlight, the angle of the sun, average temperature, and rainfall. Soil is of primary concern, and proper drainage is a requisite. The right amount of sun ripens the grapes properly to give them the sugar/acid balance that makes the difference between fair, good, and great wine.

There are five important factors in winemaking:

1. Geographic location   **2.** Soil   **3.** Weather   **4.** Grapes
            5. Vinification (the actual winemaking process)

Does it matter which types of grapes are planted?

Yes, it does. Traditionally, many grape varieties produce better wines when planted in certain locations. For example, most red grapes need a longer growing season than do white grapes, and red grapes are usually planted in warmer (more southerly) locations. In colder northern regions—in Germany and northern France, for instance—most vineyards are planted with white grapes. In the warmer regions of Italy, Spain, and Portugal, the red grape thrives.

Vines are planted during their dormant periods, usually in the months of April or May. A vine doesn't usually produce grapes suitable for winemaking until the third year. (Don't forget that the seasons in the Southern Hemisphere—Australia and Chile, for example—are reversed.) Most vines will continue to produce good-quality grapes for up to 40 years.

When's the harvest?

Grapes are picked when they reach the proper sugar/acid ratio for the style of wine the vintner wants to produce. Go to a vineyard in June and taste one of the small green grapes. Your mouth will pucker because the grape is so tart and acidic. Return to the same vineyard—even to that same vine—in September or October, and the grapes will taste sweet. All those months of sun have given sugar to the grape as a result of photosynthesis. "Brix" is the winemaker's measure of sugar in grapes.

June
3% acid
0 Brix

July
2.3% acid
10 Brix

August
1.7% acid
15 Brix

Harvest
September
0.9% acid
22 Brix

What effect does weather have on the grapes?

Weather can interfere with the quality of the harvest, as well as with its quantity. In the spring, as vines emerge from dormancy, a sudden frost may stop the flowering, thereby reducing the yields. An April frost in Bordeaux destroyed over 50% of 1991's grape harvest. Even a strong windstorm can affect the grapes adversely at this crucial time. Several years ago in Burgundy, certain villages were pelted by a 15-minute hailstorm. Its effects will not soon be forgotten—it caused almost $2 million worth of damage. Not enough rain, too much rain, or rain at the wrong time can also wreak havoc.

Rain just before the harvest will swell the grapes with water, diluting the juice and making thin, watery wines. Lack of rain, as in the drought period in California's North Coast counties in the late 1980s, will affect the balance of wines for those years. A severe drop in temperature may affect the vines even outside the growing season. Case in point: the winter of 1993–94, which visited unusually bitter cold on the wine regions of New York State. The result was a severe loss of production for the following year, particularly in those vineyards planted with the less-than-hardy European grape varieties.

What can the vineyard owner do in the case of adverse weather?

A number of countermeasures are available to the grower. Some of these measures are used while the grapes are on the vine; others are part of the winemaking process.

Problem	Results In	Solution
Frost	Reduced yield	Various frost protection methods: giant flamethrowers to warm vines
Not enough sun	Unripe grapes	Chaptalization (the addition of sugar to the must—fresh grape juice—during fermentation)
Too much rain	Thin, watery wines	Move vineyard to drier climate
Mildew	Rot	Spray with copper sulfate
Phylloxera	Dead vines	Graft vines onto resistant rootstock
Drought	Scorched grapes	Irrigate or pray for rain

What's Phylloxera?

Phylloxera, a grape louse, is one of the grapevine's worst enemies, since it eventually kills the entire plant. An epidemic infestation in the 1870s came close to destroying all the vineyards of Europe. Luckily, the roots of native American vines were immune to this louse. After this was discovered, all the European vines were pulled up and grafted onto phylloxera-resistant American rootstocks. California vineyard owners in the North Coast counties are now having problems with phylloxera in their grapevines.

Can white wine be made from red grapes?

Yes. The color of wine comes entirely from the grape skins. By removing the skins immediately after picking, no color is imparted to the wine, and it will be white. In the Champagne region of France, a large percentage of the grapes grown are red, yet most of the resulting wine is white. California's White Zinfandel is made from red Zinfandel grapes.

What's tannin, and is it desirable in wine?

Tannin is a natural substance that comes from the skins, stems, and pips of the grapes, and even from the wooden barrels in which certain wines are aged. It acts as a preservative; without it, certain wines wouldn't continue to improve in the bottle. In young wines, tannin can be very astringent and make the wine taste bitter. Generally, red wines have a higher level of tannin than do whites, because red grapes are usually left to ferment on their skins.

Is acidity desirable in wine?

All wine will have a certain amount of acid. Winemakers try to have a balance of fruitiness ("fruit") and acidity. In general, white wines have more acidity than do reds. An overly acidic wine is usually described as tart, sour, or acidic.

What's meant by "vintage"? Why is one year considered better than another?

A vintage indicates the year the grapes were harvested, so every year is a vintage year. A vintage chart reflects the weather conditions for various years. Better weather results in a better rating for the vintage.

Are all wines meant to be aged?

No. It's a common misconception that all wines improve with age. In fact, more than 90 percent of all the wines made in the world are meant to be consumed within one year, and less than 1% of the world's wines are meant to be aged for more than 10 years.

How is wine production regulated worldwide?

Each major wine-producing country has government-sponsored control agencies and laws that regulate all aspects of wine production and set certain minimum standards which must be observed. Here are some examples:

FRANCE: Appellation d'Origine Contrôlée (A.O.C.)

ITALY: Denominazione di Origine Controllata (D.O.C.)

UNITED STATES: Bureau of Alcohol, Tobacco, and Firearms (B.A.T.F.)

GERMANY: Ministry of Agriculture

SPAIN: Denominación de Origen (D.O.)

ON TASTING WINE

You can read all the books (and there are plenty) written on wine to become more knowledgeable on the subject, but you should *taste* wines to truly enhance your understanding. Reading covers the more academic side of wine, while tasting is more enjoyable and practical. A little of each will do you the most good.

Believe me, *books* have been written just on how to taste wine. You are about to learn the necessary steps. You may wish to follow them with a glass of wine in hand.

Wine tasting can be broken down into five basic steps: Color, Swirl, Smell, Taste, and Savor.

COLOR—

The best way to get an idea of the color of the wine is to get a white background—a napkin or a linen tablecloth—and hold the glass of wine in front of it. The range of colors that you may see depends, of course, on whether you're tasting a white or red wine. Here are the colors for both:

White Wine	Red Wine
pale yellow-green	purple
straw yellow	ruby
yellow-gold	red
gold	brick red
old gold	red-brown
yellow-brown	brown
maderized	
brown	

Color tells you a lot about the wine. For instance, white wines, as they get older, gain color. Red wines, on the other hand, as they get older, lose color.

Since we start with the white wines, I'll tell you three reasons why a white wine may have more color:

1. It's older.

2. *Different grape varieties give different color.* (For example, Chardonnay usually gives off a deeper color than does Riesling.)

3. The wine was aged in wood.

In class, I always begin by asking my students what color the wine is. It's not unusual to hear that some believe that the wine is pale yellow-green, while others say it's gold. Everyone begins with the same wine in front of him, but there are several different perceptions of color. So you can imagine what happens when we actually *taste* the wine!

swirl—

Why do we swirl the wine? To allow oxygen to get into the wine: Swirling releases the esters, ethers, and aldehydes which combine with oxygen to yield the bouquet of the wine. In other words, swirling aerates the wine and gives you a better smell.

Everyone does a great job swirling wine. You can do it any way you want—with your left had, your right hand, with two fingers, behind your back. . . . But I must warn you right now: You will start swirling everything—your milk, soft drinks, your morning coffee!

smell—

This is the most important part of wine tasting. You can only perceive four tastes—sweet, sour, bitter, and salt—but you can smell over 1,000 different scents. Now that you've swirled the wine and released the bouquet, I want you to smell the wine at least three times. You will find that the third smell will give you more information than the first smell did. What does the wine smell like? What type of *nose* does it have? The "nose" is a word that wine tasters use to describe the bouquet and aroma of the wine. Smell is a very important step in the tasting process that people simply don't spend enough time on.

Pinpointing the nose of the wine helps you to identify certain characteristics. The problem here is that many people in class want *me* to tell *them* what the wine smells like. Since I prefer not to use pretentious words, I may say that the wine smells like a French white Burgundy. Still, I find that this doesn't satisfy the majority of the class. They want to know more. I ask these people to describe what steak and onions smell like. They answer, "Like steak and onions." See what I mean?

The best way to learn what your own preferences are for styles of wine is to "memorize" the smell of the individual grape varieties. For white, just try to memorize the three major grape varieties: Chardonnay, Sauvignon Blanc, and Riesling. Keep smelling them, and smelling them, and smelling them until you can identify the differences, one from the other. For the reds it's a little more difficult, but you still can take three major grape varieties: Pinot Noir, Merlot, and Cabernet Sauvignon. Try to memorize those smells without using flowery words, and you'll understand what I'm talking about.

For those in the wine school who remain unconvinced, I hand out a list of 500 different words commonly used to describe wine. Here is a small excerpt:

acetic	character	legs	seductive
aftertaste	corky	light	short
aroma	delicate	maderized	soft
astringent	developed	mature	stalky
austere	earthy	metallic	sulphury
baked-burnt	finish	mouldy	tart
balanced	flat	nose	thin
big-full-heavy	fresh	nutty	tired
bitter	grapey	off	vanilla
body	green	oxidized	woody
bouquet	hard	pétillant	yeasty
bright	hot	rich	young

Another question inevitably comes up. People often ask me, "What kind of wine do *you* like?" I'd have to say I like my wine bright, rich, mature, developed, seductive, and with nice legs.

Another interesting point is that you're more likely to recognize some of the defects of a wine through your sense of smell. Following is a list of some of the negative smells in wine:

Smell	Why
Vinegar	Too much acetic acid in wine
Sherry	Oxidation
Cork (dank wet cellar smell, sometimes mouldy)	Wine absorbs taste of defective cork
Sulphur (burnt matches)	Too much sulphur dioxide

Sulphur dioxide is used in many ways in winemaking. It kills bacteria in wine, prevents unwanted fermentation, and acts as a preservative. However, a good wine should never have the sense of sulphur dioxide, which causes a burning and itching sensation in your nose.

TASTE—

To many people, tasting wine means taking a sip and swallowing immediately. This isn't tasting. Tasting is something you do with your taste buds. And remember, you have taste buds all over your mouth. They're on both sides of the tongue, underneath, on the tip, and they extend to the back of your throat. If you do what many people do, you take a gulp of wine and bypass all of those important taste buds.

What should you think about when tasting wine?

Be aware of the most important sensations of taste and where they occur on your tongue and in your mouth. As I mentioned earlier, you can only perceive four tastes: sweet, sour, bitter, and salt (but there's no salt in wine, so we're down to three). Bitterness in wine is usually created by high alcohol and high tannin. Sweetness only occurs in wines that have some residual sugar left over after fermentation. Sour (sometimes called "tart") indicates the acidity in wine.

Sweetness—Found on the tip of the tongue. If there is any sweetness in a wine whatsoever, you'll get it right away.

Fruit and Varietal Characteristics—Found in the middle of the tongue.

Acidity—Found at the sides of the tongue, the cheek area, and the back of the throat. It's most commonly present in white wines and some lighter-style red wines.

Tannin—The sensation of tannin begins in the middle of the tongue. Tannin frequently exists in red wines or wood-aged white wines. When the wines are too young, it dries the palate to excess. If there's a lot of tannin in the wine, the tannin can actually coat your whole mouth.

Aftertaste—This is the overall taste and balance of the components of the wine that lingers in your mouth. How long does the balance last? Usually a sign of a high-quality wine is a long, pleasing aftertaste. The taste of many of the great wines lasts anywhere from 1 minute to 3 minutes, with all of their components in harmony.

Savor—

After you've had a chance to taste the wine, sit back for a few moments and savor it. Think about what you just experienced and ask yourself the following questions to help focus your impressions. Was the wine:

Light, medium, or full-bodied? (Think: skim milk, whole milk, heavy cream.)

For a white wine: How was the acidity? Very little, just right, or too much?

For red wine: Is the tannin in the wine too strong or astringent? Is it pleasing? Or is it missing?

How long did the balance of the components last?

Is the wine ready to drink?

To your taste, is the wine worth the price?

What is the strongest component (residual sugar, fruit, acid, tannin)?

What kind of food must go with the wine?

This brings us to the most important point. The first thing you should consider after you've tasted a wine is whether or not you like it. Is it your style?

You can compare tasting wine to browsing in an art gallery. You wander from room to room looking at the paintings. Your first impression tells whether you like one or not. Once you decide you like a piece of art, you want to know more: Who was the artist? What is the history behind the work? How was it done? And so it is with wine. Usually, once oenophiles discover a new wine that they like, they have to know all about it—the winemaker, the grapes, exactly where the crop was planted, the blend, if any, and the history behind the wine.

How do you know if a wine is good or not?

The definition of a good wine is one that you enjoy. Do not let others dictate taste to you!

When's a wine ready to drink?

This is one of the most frequently asked questions at the Windows on the World Wine School. The answer is very simple—when all components of the wine are in balance to your particular taste.

> For further reading:
> Michael Broadbent's
> *Pocket Guide to Wine Tasting.*

The One-Minute Wine Expert Tasting Sheet

WINE _____

DATE TESTED _____

COLOR _____

SMELL (Aroma, Bouquet) _____

60-SECOND WINE TASTING

0 - 15 SUGAR SHOCK _____

15 - 30 BALANCE OF COMPONENTS
HARMONIZING _____

30 - 45 FORMULATE YOUR OPINION ____

45 - 60 FORMULATE YOUR OPINION ____

____ LIGHT-BODIED   ____ MEDIUM-BODIED   ____ FULL-BODIED

RESIDUAL
SUGAR: LOW ↓ __   BALANCED ↔ __   HIGH ↑ __

FRUIT: LOW ↓ __   BALANCED ↔ __   HIGH ↑ __

ACID: LOW ↓ __   BALANCED ↔ __   HIGH ↑ __

TANNIN: LOW ↓ __   BALANCED ↔ __   HIGH ↑ __

DRINKABILITY _____

READY TO DRINK ____ MORE TIME ____ PAST ITS PRIME ____

COST _____

PERSONAL RATING/COMMENTS _____

_____

FOOD SUGGESTIONS _____

_____

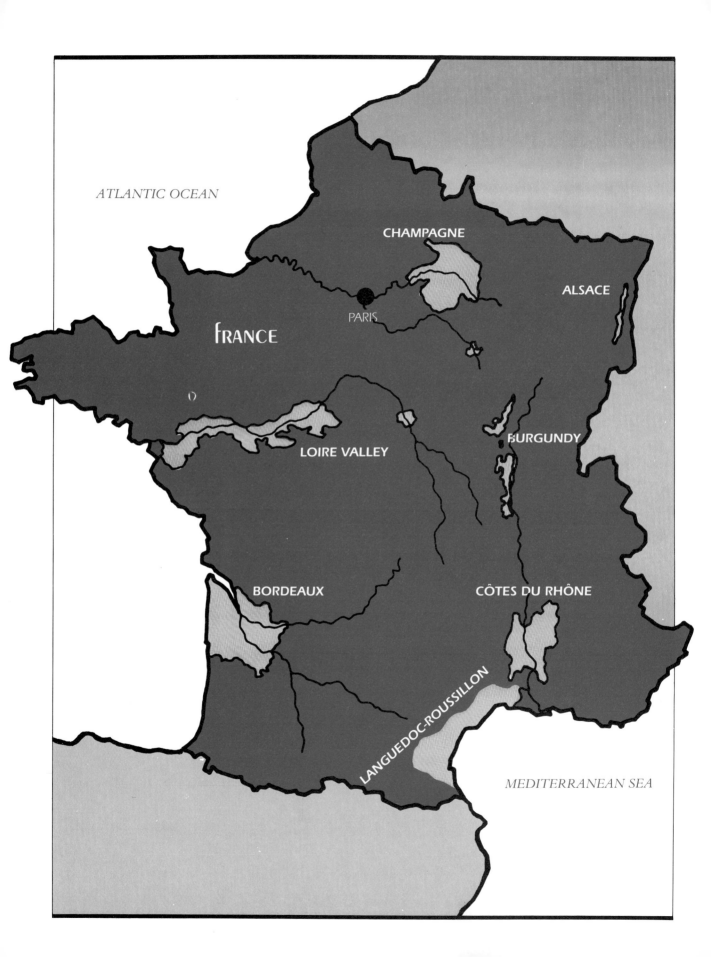

THE WHITE WINES of FRANCE

UNDERSTANDING FRENCH WINE

Before we begin our first "class," "The White Wines of France," I think you should know a few important points about all French wines. Take a look at a map of France to get familiar with the main wine-producing areas. As we progress, you'll understand why geography is so important.

Here's a quick rundown of which areas produce which kinds of wine:

Champagne—sparkling wine

Loire Valley—mostly white

Alsace—mostly white

Burgundy—red and white

Bordeaux—red and white

Côtes du Rhône—mostly red

Languedoc-Roussillon—red and white

I'm sure that you've had a French wine at one time or another. Why? Because French wines have the reputation of being among the best. There's a reason for this, and it goes back to quality control.

French winemaking is regulated by strict government laws that are set up by the *Appellation d'Origine Contrôlée*. If you don't want to say "Appellation d'Origine Contrôlée" all the time, you can simply say the "A.O.C." This is the first of many wine "lingo" abbreviations you'll learn in this book.

Only 35% of all French wines are worthy of A.O.C. designation.

21

A.O.C.

Established in the 1930s, the Appellation d'Origine Contrôlée laws set *minimum* requirements for each wine-producing area in France. The A.O.C. laws also can help you to decipher French wine labels, since the A.O.C. controls the following:

	Example	**Example**
1. Geographic origin	Chablis	Pommard
2. Grape variety: Which grapes can be planted where.	Chardonnay only	Pinot Noir only
3. Minimum alcohol content: This varies depending upon the particular area where the grapes are grown.	10%	10.5%
4. Vinegrowing practices: For example, a vintner can produce only so much wine per acre.	40 hectolitres/ hectare	35 hectolitres/ hectare

Hectare—metric measure; 1 hectare = 2.471 acres.

Hectolitre—metric measure; 1 hectolitre = 26.42 U.S. gallons.

There are more than 350 A.O.C. wines.

The region most active in the production of Vin de Pays varietal wines is the Midi, also called Languedoc-Rousillon, in southwest France. Called in the past the "wine lake" because of the vast quantities of anonymous wine made there, the Midi now ships hundreds of thousands of cases of good-quality, affordable varietal wines offering good value for the money.

Why would Georges Duboeuf, Louis Latour and many other famous winemakers start wineries in the Midi? For one thing, Midi vineyard land is much cheaper than land in places such as Burgundy or Bordeaux, so the wine-makers can produce moderately priced wines and still get a good return on their investment.

Appellation d'Origine Vins Délimités de Qualité Supérieure—Known as A.O.V.D.Q.S., this is a step below A.O.C. wines and represents 1% of production.

Vins de Pays—This is a category that's growing in importance. A 1979 French legal decision liberalized the rules for this category, permitting the use of non-traditional grapes in certain regions, and even allowing vintners to label wines with the varietal name rather than with the regional name. For exporters to the American market, where consumers are becoming accustomed to buying wines by grape variety—Merlot or Chardonnay, for example—this change makes their wines much easier to sell.

Vins de Table—These are ordinary, simple table wines and represent almost 35 percent of all wines produced in France.

Most French wine is meant to be consumed as a simple beverage. Many of the *vins de table* are marketed under proprietary names and are the French equivalent of California jug wines. Don't be surprised if you go into a grocery store in France to buy wine and find it in a plastic wine container with no label on it! You can see the color through the plastic—either red, white, or rosé—but the only marking on the container is the alcohol content, ranging from 9 to 14 percent. You choose your wine depending on what you have to do during the rest of the day.

When you buy wines, keep these distinctions in mind, because there's not only a difference in quality, but also in price.

What are the four major white-wine-producing regions of France?

Alsace

Loire Valley

Bordeaux

Burgundy

Let's start with Alsace and the Loire Valley, because these are the two French regions truly known for white wines. As you can see from the map at the beginning of this chapter, Alsace, the Loire Valley, and Chablis (a white-wine-producing region of Burgundy) have one thing in common: They're all located in the northern region of France. These areas produce white wines predominantly, because of the shorter growing season and the cooler climate, both of which are best suited for growing white grapes.

ALSACE

I often find that people are confused about the difference between wines from Alsace and those from Germany. Why do you suppose this is?

First of all, Alsace and Germany grow the same grape varieties. When you think of Riesling, what are your associations? You'll probably answer *Germany* and *sweetness*. That's a very typical response. However, after the winemaker from Alsace harvests his Riesling, he makes his wine much differently from the wine of his German counterpart. The winemaker from Alsace ferments every bit of the sugar in the grape, while in Germany, the winemaker adds a small amount of the naturally sweet unfermented grape juice back into the wine, which creates the typical German style. Ninety-nine percent of all Alsace wines are totally dry.

Another fundamental difference between wine from Alsace and wine from Germany is the alcohol content. Wine from Alsace has 11 to 12 percent alcohol, while most German wine has a mere 8 to 9 percent.

Just to confuse you a bit more, both wines are bottled in similarly shaped bottles that are tall with a tapering neck.

Famous non-A.O.C. French wines that are available in the United States include: Partager, Valbon, Moreau, Boucheron, Chantefleur, and René Junot.

Champagne is another major white-wine producer, but that's a chapter in itself.

From 1871 to 1919, Alsace was part of Germany.

All wines produced in Alsace are A.O.C.-designated wines, and represent nearly 20% of all A.O.C. white wines in France.

23

What are the white grapes grown in Alsace?

The four grapes you should know are:

Riesling—accounts for 23 percent
Gewurztraminer—accounts for 19 percent
Pinot Blanc—accounts for 20 percent
Tokay–Pinot Gris—accounts for 7 percent

What type of wine is produced in Alsace?

As we mentioned earlier, virtually all the Alsace wines are dry. Riesling is the major grape planted in Alsace, and it is responsible for the highest-quality wines of the region. The other wine Alsace is known for is Gewurztraminer, which is in a class by itself. Most people either love it or hate it, because Gewurztraminer has a very distinctive style. "Gewürz" is the German word for "spice," which aptly describes the wine.

Pinot Blanc is a "new-style" wine for the region, and it's becoming increasingly popular with the growers of Alsace.

How should I select an Alsace wine?

Two factors are important in choosing a wine from Alsace: the grape variety and the reputation and style of the shipper. Some of the most reliable shippers are:

Hugel & Fils

F. E. Trimbach

Léon Beyer

Dopff "Au Moulin"

Domaine Zind-Humbrecht

Alsace produces 8% red wines. These generally are consumed in the region and are rarely exported.

Wine labelling in Alsace is different from other regions administered by the A.O.C., because Alsace is the only region that labels its wine by specific grape variety. All Alsace wines that put the name of the grape on the label must contain 100% of that grape.

In the last ten years, there have been more Pinot Blanc and Riesling grapes planted in Alsace than any other variety.

Why are the shippers so important?

Because the majority of the landholders in Alsace don't grow enough grapes for it to be economically feasible to produce and market their own wine. Instead, they sell their grapes to a shipper who produces, bottles, and markets the wine under his own name. The art of making high-quality wine lies in the selection of grapes made by each shipper.

What are the different quality levels of Alsace wine?

The vast majority of the wine is a shipper's varietal: A very small percentage is labelled with a specific vineyard's name, especially in the appellation "Alsace Grand Cru." Some wines are also labelled "Réserve" or "Réserve Personelle," which terms are not legally defined. Their importance is determined by the shipper's reputation.

There are 35,000 acres of grapes planted in Alsace, but the average plot of land for each grower is only five acres.

Sometimes you'll see "grand cru" on an Alsace label. This wine can be made only from the best grape varieties of Alsace. With the 1993 vintage, 25 vineyards were elevated to grand cru status, doubling the total number of Alsace grands crus. The first 25 grands crus were adopted in 1983.

Should I lay down my Alsace wines for long aging?

In general, most Alsace wines are made to be consumed young—that is, one to five years after they're bottled. As in any fine-wine area, there is a small percentage of great wines produced in Alsace that may be aged for ten years or more.

What are the trends in Alsace wine over the last ten years?

What I've learned over the last ten years is that the more I drink Alsace wines, the more I like them. They're fresh, they're "clean," they're easy to drink, they're very compatible with food.

I think Riesling is still the best grape, but Pinot Blanc, which is lighter in style, is a perfect apéritif wine at a very good price.

Most Alsace wines are very affordable, of good quality, and are available in most markets.

In 1994, about 70,000 cases of Alsace wine were sold in the United States.

The Alsace region has little rainfall, especially during the grape harvest, and the town of Colmar, the Alsace wine center, is the second-driest city in France. That's why they say a "one-shirt harvest" will be a good vintage.

> ## Best Bets for Recent Vintages of Alsace
> ### 1990 1991 1992 1993

wine and food

During a visit to Alsace, I spoke with two of the region's best-known producers to find out which types of food they enjoy with Alsace wines. Here's what they prefer:

Jean Hugel—"With Riesling, fish in a white sauce or butter sauce. With Gewurztraminer, smoked salmon, turkey, or Chinese food."

FRENCH TABLE WINE
ALSACE
APPELLATION ALSACE CONTRÔLÉE

DEPUIS   1639

GEWURZTRAMINER "HUGEL"
750 ml ℮
MISE EN BOUTEILLE PAR HUGEL ET FILS · RIQUEWIHR · ALSACE · FRANCE

Alsace is also known for its fruit brandies—"eaux-de-vie":
Framboise—raspberries
Kirsch—cherries
Mirabelle—yellow plums
Fraise—strawberries
Poire—pears

For the Tourist:
Visit the beautiful wine village of Riquewihr, whose buildings date from the fifteenth-sixteenth century.

For further reading:
Alsace by S. F. Hallgarten; Alsace by Pamela Van Dyke Price.

Mr. Hugel described Pinot Blanc as, "round, soft, not aggressive . . . an all-purpose wine . . . can be used as an apéritif, with all kinds of *pâté* and *charcuterie,* and also with hamburgers. Perfect for brunch—not too sweet or flowery."

Hubert Trimbach—"Riesling with fish—blue trout with a light sauce." He recommends Gewurztraminer as an apéritif, or with *foie gras* or any *pâté* at the end of the meal; with Muenster cheese, or a stronger cheese such as Roquefort.

25

Loire Valley

Starting at the city of Nantes, a bit upriver from the Atlantic Ocean, this valley stretches inland for 600 miles along the Loire River.

There are two grape varieties you should be familiar with:

Sauvignon Blanc   **Chenin Blanc**

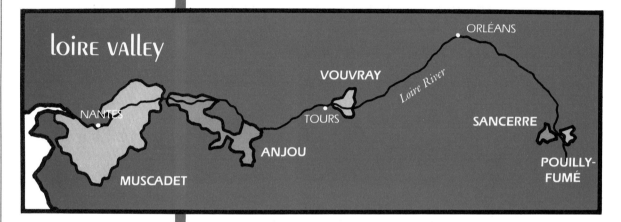

Rather than choosing by grape variety and shipper, as you would in Alsace, choose a Loire Valley wine by style and vintage. Here are the main styles:

Pouilly-Fumé—a dry wine that has the most body and concentration of all the Loire Valley wines. It's made with 100 percent Sauvignon Blanc.

Muscadet—A light, dry wine, made from 100 percent Melon grape.

Sancerre—Striking a balance between full-bodied Pouilly-Fumé and light-bodied Muscadet, it's made with 100 percent Sauvignon Blanc.

Vouvray—The "chameleon"; it can be dry, semisweet, or sweet. It's made from 100 percent Chenin Blanc.

How did Pouilly-Fumé get its name, and what does "Fumé" mean?

Many people ask me if Pouilly-Fumé is smoked, because they automatically associate the word "fumé" with smoke. One of the many theories about the origin of the word comes from the white morning mist that blankets the area. As the sun burns off the mist, it looks as if smoke is rising.

When are the wines ready to drink?

Generally, Loire Valley wines are meant to be consumed young. The exception is a sweet Vouvray, which can be laid down for a longer time.

Here are more specific guidelines:

Pouilly-Fumé—three to five years
Sancerre—two to three years
Muscadet—one to two years.

What are the trends in Loire Valley wines over the last ten years?

Ten years ago, at Windows on the World, we started promoting Sancerre over Pouilly-Fumé. Both are made with the same grape variety, but the Sancerre was less expensive. Today, with a demand for both wines, they have become much more expensive, with Sancerre sometimes even more expensive than Pouilly-Fumé.

Muscadet, on the other hand, remains a good value. In fact, I think these wines are being made even better than they were ten years ago.

Best Bets for Recent Vintages of Loire Valley
1990   1993

WINE AND food

Baron Patrick Ladoucette—Owner of Ladoucette Pouilly-Fumé (and incidentally the largest producer of Pouilly-Fumé)—recommends the following wine and food combinations:

Pouilly-Fumé—"Smoked salmon, turbot with hollandaise; white meat chicken; veal with cream sauce."

Sancerre—"Shellfish, simple food of the sea, because Sancerre is drier than Pouilly-Fumé."

Muscadet—"All you have to do is look at the map to see where Muscadet is made: by the sea where the main fare is shellfish, clams, and oysters."

Vouvray—"A nice semidry wine to have with fruit and cheese."

Marquis Robert de Goulaine—"Muscadet is good with a huge variety of excellent and fresh 'everyday' foods, including all the seafood from the Atlantic Ocean, the fish from the river—pike, for instance—game, poultry, and cheese (mainly goat cheese). Of course, there is a *must* in the region of Nantes: freshwater fish with the world-famous butter sauce, the *beurre blanc,* invented at the turn of the century by Clémence, who happened to be the chef at Goulaine. Finally, remember that most of the Loire wines, and specifically Muscadet, can be drunk on their own, as an apéritif or during a party. Muscadet with a dash of crème de cassis (black currant) is a wonderful way to welcome friends!"

If you see the word sur-lie on a Muscadet wine label, it means that the wine was aged with its sediment.

27

THE WHITE WINES
of bordeAUX

When people think of white Bordeaux wines, they normally think of the major areas of Graves or Pessac-Léognan, but some of the best value/quality white wines produced in Bordeaux come from the area called Entre-Deux-Mers.

Doesn't Bordeaux always mean red wine?

That's a misconception. Actually, two of the five major areas of Bordeaux are known for their excellent white wines—Graves and Sauternes. Sauternes is world-famous for its sweet white wine.

The major white grape varieties used in both areas are:

Sémillon   **Sauvignon Blanc**

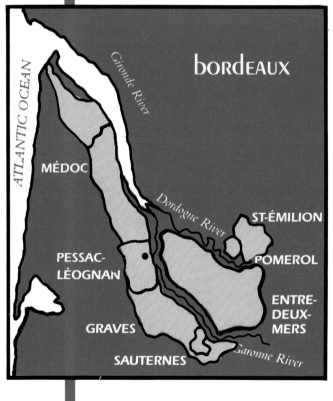

The word "Graves" means gravel–the type of soil found in the region.

Two-thirds of Bordeaux wines are red and one-third are white.

GRAVES

How are the white Graves wines classified?

There are two levels of quality distinction:

Graves   **Pessac-Léognan**

The most basic Graves is simply called "Graves." The best wines are produced in Pessac-Léognan. Both are regional wines. Those labelled "Graves" are from the southern portion of the region closest to Sauternes, while Pessac-Léognan is in the northern half of the region, next to the city of Bordeaux. The best wines are known by the name of a particular château, a special vineyard that produces the best-quality grapes. The grapes grown for these wines enjoy better soil and better growing conditions overall. The classified château wines and the regional wines of Graves are always dry.

How should I select a Graves wine?

My best recommendation would be to purchase a classified château wine. Here they are:

Château Bouscaut★
Château Carbonnieux★
Domaine de Chevalier
Château Couhins
Château La Louvière★
Château La Tour-Martillac
Château Laville-Haut-Brion
Château Malartic-Lagravière
Château Olivier★

★The largest producers and the easiest to find.

The wine production of Graves is divided evenly between red and white.

Classified white château wines are hard to find, since they make up only 3% of the total production of white Graves.

What are the trends in the white wines of Bordeaux over the last ten years?

Some of the major changes in French white wines have occurred in the Bordeaux region. The winemakers have changed the style through more modern winemaking techniques, as well as being more careful with their selection in the vineyard, thus resulting in a much higher quality of white Bordeaux wines.

The style of classified white château wines varies with the ratio of Sauvignon Blanc and Sémillon used. Château Olivier, for example, is made with 65% Sémillon, and Château Carbonnieux with 65% Sauvignon Blanc.

Best Bets for Recent Vintages of White Graves
1989   1990   1993

WINE ANd food

Denise Lurton-Moulle (Château La Louvière, Château Bonnet)—With Château La Louvière Blanc, grilled sea bass with a beurre blanc, shad roe, goat cheese soufflé. With Château Bonnet Blanc, oysters on the half-shell, fresh crab salad, mussels and clams.

Antony Perrin (Château Carbonnieux)—With a young Château Carbonnieux Blanc, chilled lobster consommé, or shellfish such as oysters, scallops or grilled shrimps. With an older Carbonnieux, a traditional sauced fish course or with a goat cheese.

Jean-Jacques de Bethmann (Château Olivier)—Oysters, lobster, *Rouget du Bassin d'Archon*.

There's more Sémillon planted in Bordeaux than there is Sauvignon Blanc.

SAUTERNES/BARSAC

All French Sauternes are sweet, meaning that not all the grape sugar has turned into alcohol during fermentation. A dry French Sauternes doesn't exist. The Barsac district, adjacent to Sauternes, has the option of choosing between Barsac or Sauternes as its appellation.

What are the main grape varieties in Sauternes?

Sémillon
Sauvignon Blanc

If the same grapes are used for both the dry Graves and the sweet Sauternes, how do you explain the extreme difference in styles?

First and most important, the best Sauternes is made primarily with the Sémillon grape. Second, to make Sauternes, the winemaker leaves the grapes on the vine longer. He waits for a mould called *Botrytis cinerea* (noble rot) to form. When this "noble rot" forms on the grapes, the water within them evaporates and they shrivel. Sugar becomes concentrated as the grapes "raisinate." Then, during the winemaking process, not all of the sugar is allowed to ferment into alcohol: hence, the high-residual sugar.

What are the trends in Sauternes over the last ten years?

Sauternes is still producing one of the greatest sweet wines in the world. With the great vintages of the 1980s, you'll be able to find excellent regional Sauternes, if you buy from the best shippers. These wines represent a good value for your money, considering the labor involved in production.

Other sweet-wine producing in Bordeaux: Ste-Croix-du-Mont Loupiac

Sauternes is expensive to produce because several pickings must be completed before the crop is entirely harvested. The harvest can last into November.

Sauternes is a wine you can age. In fact, most classified château wines in good vintages can easily age for ten to thirty years.

Doesn't Château d'Yquem make a dry white wine? Yes, they do, but the law states that a dry Sauternes must be labelled as Bordeaux.

Château d'Yquem
Lur-Saluces
1975

How are Sauternes classified?

First Great Growth—Grand Premier Cru
Château d'Yquem★

First Growth—Premiers Crus
Château La Tour Blanche★
Château Lafaurie-Peyraguey★
Clos Haut-Peyraguey★
Château de Rayne-Vigneau★
Château Suduiraut★
Château Coutet★ (Barsac)
Château Climens★ (Barsac)
Château Guiraud★
Château Rieussec★
Château Rabaud-Promis
Château Sigalas-Rabaud★

Second Growths—Deuxièmes Crus
Château Myrat (Barsac)
Château Doisy-Daëne (Barsac)
Château Doisy-Védrines★ (Barsac)
Château Doisy-Dubroca
Château d'Arche
Château Filhot★
Château Broustet (Barsac)
Château Nairac★ (Barsac)
Château Caillou (Barsac)
Château Suau (Barsac)
Château de Malle★
Château Romer du Hayot★
Château Lamothe

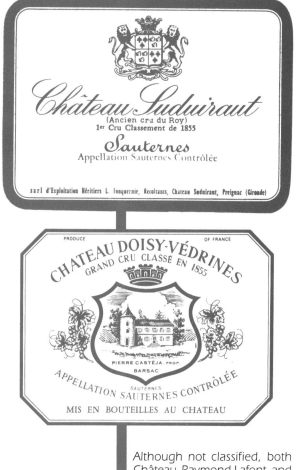

Although not classified, both Château Raymond-Lafont and Château Largues are owned by Château d'Yquem.

★These are the wines that are most readily available in the United States and are of consistent high quality. Many of the other châteaus are very small, and they don't export wine to the United States.

Best Bets for Vintages of Sauternes
1967 1970 1971 1975 1976 1979
1980 1981 1983 1986 1988 1989 1990

How do I buy Sauternes?

It's similar to buying the wines of Graves. You may buy a regional or a château wine. A regional wine, simply labelled Sauternes, may be a good buy, but it won't have the same intensity of flavor as a classified château wine. One other very important consideration is the vintage: In Sauternes, only buy the best years.

When buying regional Sauternes look for these reputable shippers: Baron Philippe de Rothschild and B&G.

31

Just Desserts

My students always ask me, "What do you serve with Sauternes?" Here's a little lesson I learned when I first encountered the wines of Sauternes.

Many years ago, when I was visiting the Sauternes region, I was invited to one of the châteaus for dinner. Upon arrival, my group was offered appetizers of *foie gras*, and, to my surprise, Sauternes was served with it. All of the books that I had ever read said you should serve drier wines first and sweeter wines later. But since I was a guest, I thought it best not to question my host's selection.

When we sat down for the first dinner course, we were once again served a Sauternes. This continued through the main course—which happened to be rack of lamb—when another Sauternes was served.

I thought for sure our host would serve a great old red Bordeaux with the cheese course, but I was wrong again. With the Roquefort cheese was served a very old Sauternes.

With dessert soon on its way, I got used to the idea of having a dinner with Sauternes, and waited with anticipation for the final choice. You can imagine my surprise when a red Bordeaux—Château Lafite-Rothschild—was served with dessert!

My point is that Sauternes doesn't have to be served *only* with dessert. Actually, all of the Sauternes went well with the courses, because all of the sauces complemented the wine and food.

By the way, the only wine that *didn't* go well with dinner was the Château Lafite-Rothschild with dessert, but we drank it anyway.

Perhaps this anecdote will inspire you to serve Sauternes with everything. Personally, I prefer to enjoy Sauternes by itself; I'm not a believer in the dessert wine category. This dessert wine is dessert in itself.

Château Rieussec is owned by the Domaine owners of Château Lafitte Rothschild.

THE WHITE WINES of burgundy

Where's Burgundy?

Burgundy is a region located in central eastern France. Its true fame is as a wine-producing area.

What's Burgundy?

This may sound like a silly question, but many people are confused about what a Burgundy really is because the name is often misused on the market.

For our purposes, Burgundy is one of the major wine-producing regions that holds an A.O.C. designation in France. *Burgundy is not a synonym for red wine, although many red wines are simply labelled "Burgundy."* Many of these Burgundy wines are ordinary table wines. They may come from California, South Africa, Australia, or Chile, and bear little resemblance to the styles of authentic French Burgundy wines.

The largest city in Burgundy is known not for its wines, but for another world-famous product. The city is Dijon, and the product is mustard.

"You mean France makes burgundy, too?"

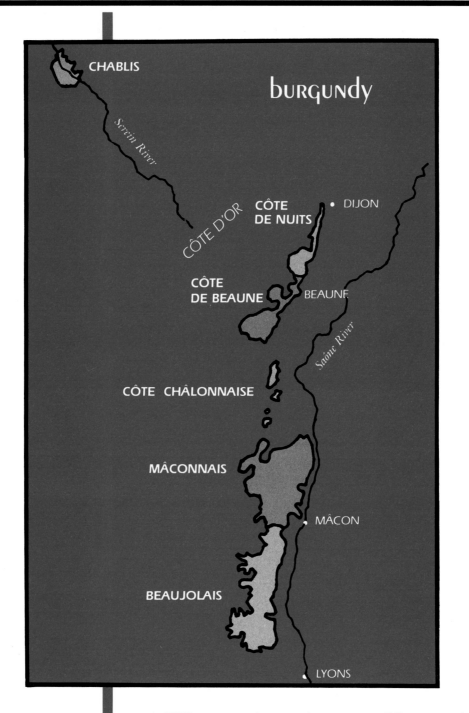

What are the main areas of Burgundy?

Chablis

Côte d'Or } **Côte de Nuits**
                  Côte de Beaune

Côte Châlonnaise

Mâconnais

Beaujolais

Although Chablis is part of the Burgundy region, it is a three-hour drive south from there to the Mâconnais area.

Before we explore Burgundy, region by region, it's important to know the types of wine that are produced there. Take a look at the chart below: It breaks down the types of wine and tells you the percentage of reds to whites.

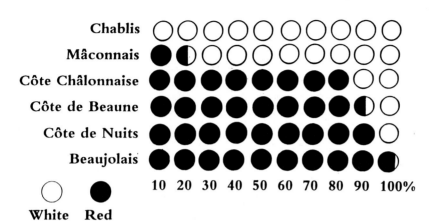

		White: 100%
Chablis		White: 100%
Mâconnais		White: 85%; Red: 15%
Côte Châlonnaise		White: 20%; Red: 80%
Côte de Beaune		White: 15%; Red: 85%
Côte de Nuits		White: 10%; Red: 90%
Beaujolais		White: 1%; Red: 99%

10 20 30 40 50 60 70 80 90 100%

○ White ● Red

Burgundy is another one of those regions that's so famous for its red wines that people sometimes forget that some of the finest white wines of France are also produced there. The three areas in Burgundy which produce world-famous white wines are:

Chablis   Côte de Beaune   Mâconnais

> If it's any comfort to you, you need to know only one white grape variety—Chardonnay. All of the great white Burgundian wine is made from 100 percent Chardonnay.

Is there only one type of white Burgundy?

Although Chardonnay is used to make all the best French white Burgundy wines, the different areas produce many different styles. Much of this has to do with where the grapes are grown and the vinification procedures. In the Chablis and Mâconnais areas, the grapes are harvested, mostly fermented, and aged in stainless-steel tanks. In the Côte de Beaune, after the grapes are harvested, a good percentage of the wines are fermented in wood. Then the wines are transferred to small oak barrels, where they age. The wood adds depth, body, flavor, and longevity to the wines.

White Burgundies have one trait in common: They are dry.

Another white grape found in the Burgundy region is the Aligoté. It is a lesser grape variety and usually the grape name appears on the label.

There are more than 250 grape growers in Chablis, but only a handful age their wine in wood.

The Story of Kir

Over the last few years, the apéritif "Kir" has become very popular. It is a mixture of white wine and cassis (made from black currants). It was the favorite drink of the former mayor of Dijon, Canon Kir, who originally mixed the sweet cassis to balance the acidity of the white Burgundy wine made from the Aligoté grape.

A Note on the Use of Wood

Each wine region in the world has its own way of producing wines. Wine was always fermented and aged in wood—until the introduction of cement tanks, glass-lined tanks, and most recently, stainless-steel tanks. Despite these technological improvements, many winemakers prefer to use the more traditional methods. For example, wines from the firm of Louis Jadot are fermented in wood as follows:

One-third of the wine is fermented in new wood.

One-third of the wine is fermented in year-old wood.

One-third of the wine is fermented in older wood.

Jadot's philosophy is that the better the vintage, the more the wood aging; the lesser the vintage, the less the wood aging. A lesser vintage wine will usually not be aged in new wood for fear the wine would be overpowered by it. The younger the wood, the more flavor and tannin it gives to the wine.

Vineyards with southeastern exposure receive the most sunlight and are therefore the most valuable.

Most premier cru wines give you the name of the vineyard on the label, but others are simply called "premier cru," which is a blend of different "cru" vineyards.

The average yield for a village wine in Burgundy is 360 gallons per acre. For the grand cru wines it is 290 gallons per acre, a noticeably larger concentration, which produces a more flavorful wine.

How are the white wines of Burgundy classified?

The type of soil and the angle and direction of the slope are the primary factors determining quality. Here are the levels of quality:

Village Wine—
Bears the name of a specific village. ($ = good)

Premier Cru—
From a specific vineyard with special characteristics, within one of the named villages. Usually a premier cru wine will list the village first and the vineyard second. ($$ = better)

Grand Cru—
From a specific vineyard which possesses the best soil and slope in the area and meets or exceeds all other requirements. In most areas of Burgundy, the village won't appear on the label—only the vineyard name is used. ($$$$ = best)

chablis

Chablis is the northernmost area in Burgundy, and it produces only white wine.

Isn't Chablis just a general term for white wine?

The name "Chablis" suffers from the same misinterpretation and overuse as does the name "Burgundy." Because the French didn't take the necessary precautions to protect the use of the name "Chablis," it's now randomly applied to many ordinary bulk wines from other countries. Chablis has come to be associated with some very undistinguished wine, *but this is not the case with French Chablis.* In fact, the French take their Chablis very seriously. There is a special classification of Chablis.

What are the quality levels of Chablis?

Petit Chablis—The most ordinary Chablis; rarely seen in the United States.

Chablis—A wine that comes from grapes grown anywhere in the Chablis district.

Chablis Premier Cru—A very good quality of Chablis that comes from specific high-quality vineyards.

Chablis Grand Cru—The highest classification of Chablis, and the most expensive because of its limited production. There are only seven vineyards in Chablis entitled to be called grand cru.

All Chablis is made of 100 percent Chardonnay.

Of these quality levels, the best price/value wine is a Chablis Premier Cru.

There are only 245 acres planted in grand cru vineyards.

Village	**Premier Cru**	**Grand Cru**

If you're interested in buying only the best Chablis, here are the seven grands crus and the most important premiers crus vineyards:

THE GRAND CRU VINEYARDS OF CHABLIS

Les Clos   Blanchots
Vaudésir   Preuses
Valmur   Grenouilles
            Bougros

THE TOP PREMIER CRU VINEYARDS OF CHABLIS

Vaillons   Fourchaume
Montée de Tonnerre   Montmains
Monts de Milieu   Côte de Vaulorent
            Lechet

What has been the most important recent change in Chablis?

The cold, northerly climate of Chablis poses a threat to the vines. Back in the late 1950s, Chablis almost went out of business because the crops were ruined by frost. Through modern technology, with improved methods of frost protection, vintners have learned to control this problem, so more wine is being produced.

The winter temperatures in some parts of Chablis can match those of Norway.

How should I buy Chablis?

The two major aspects to look for in Chablis are the shipper and the vintage. Here is a list of the most important shippers of Chablis to the United States:

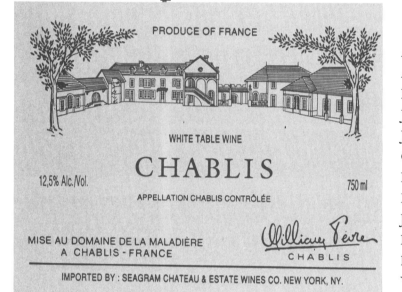

PRODUCE OF FRANCE

WHITE TABLE WINE

CHABLIS

12,5% Alc./Vol.   750 ml

APPELLATION CHABLIS CONTRÔLÉE

MISE AU DOMAINE DE LA MALADIÈRE
A CHABLIS - FRANCE

CHABLIS

IMPORTED BY : SEAGRAM CHATEAU & ESTATE WINES CO. NEW YORK, NY.

Albert Pic & Fils

A Regnard & Fils

Domaine de la Maladière

Joseph Drouhin

J. Moreau & Fils

Guy Robin

Robert Vocoret

Louis Jadot

Jean Dauvissat

René Dauvissat

François Raveneau

William Fevre

Best Bets for Recent Vintages of Chablis
1989   1991   1992

When should I drink my Chablis?

Chablis—within two years from the vintage

Premier Cru—after two but before four years

Grand Cru—after three but before five years

CÔTE DE BEAUNE

This is one of the two major areas of the Cote d'Or. Very few of the wines from this area are white, but they are some of the finest examples of dry white wine produced in the world and are considered a benchmark for winemakers everywhere.

Two important white wines of Burgundy made in limited quantity from the Côte de Nuits are Musigny Blanc and Clos Blanc de Vougeot.

Côte de Beaune

Here is a list of my favorite villages and vineyards in the Côte de Beaune that produce white wines.

Village	Premier Cru Vineyards	Grand Cru Vineyards
Aloxe-Corton		Corton-Charlemagne Charlemagne
Beaune	Clos des Mouches	None
Meursault	Les Perrières Les Genevrières La Goutte d'Or Les Charmes Blagny Poruzots	None
Puligny-Montrachet	Les Combettes Les Caillerets Les Pucelles Les Folatières Clavoillons Les Referts	Montrachet★ Bâtard-Montrachet★ Chevalier-Montrachet Bienvenue-Bâtard-Montrachet
Chassagne-Montrachet	Les Ruchottes Morgeot	Montrachet★ Bâtard-Montrachet★ Criots-Bâtard-Montrachet

★The vineyards of Bâtard-Montrachet and Montrachet overlap between the villages of Puligny-Montrachet and Chassagne-Montrachet.

The three most important villages are: Meursault, Puligny-Montrachet, and Chassagne-Montrachet. All three villages produce their wine from the same grape–100 percent Chardonnay.

The largest grand cru, in terms of production, is Corton-Charlemagne, which represents more than 50 percent of all white grand cru wines.

Village

Puligny-Montrachet

APPELLATION CONTROLÉE

Louis Latour

MIS EN BOUTEILLE PAR LOUIS LATOUR

NÉGOCIANT A BEAUNE (COTE-D'OR)

ROUALET BEAUNE

Premier Cru

Puligny-Montrachet
LES REFERTS
APPELLATION CONTROLÉE

Louis Latour

MIS EN BOUTEILLE PAR LOUIS LATOUR

NÉGOCIANT A BEAUNE (CÔTE-D'OR)

ROUALET BEAUNE

Grand Cru

Montrachet

APPELLATION CONTROLÉE

Louis Latour

MIS EN BOUTEILLE PAR LOUIS LATOUR

NÉGOCIANT A BEAUNE (COTE-D'OR)

ROUALET BEAUNE

As Robert Drouhin, a leading winemaker in Burgundy, says: "The difference between the Village wine, Puligny-Montrachet, and the Grand Cru Montrachet, is not in the type of wood used in aging or how long the wine is aged in wood. The primary difference is in the location of the vineyards, i.e., the soil and the slope of the land."

Then what makes each wine different?

In Burgundy, one of the most important factors in making a good wine is *soil*. Soil makes the difference between a Village, a Premier Cru, and a Grand Cru wine. Another major factor that makes the wines different in style is the vinification procedure the winemaker uses—the recipe. It's the same as if you were to compare the chefs at three gourmet restaurants. They may start out with the same ingredients, but it's what they do with those ingredients that matters.

Best Bets of Côte de Beaune White
1988   1989   1990   1992   1993

For the first time in decades, Burgundy had three great vintages in a row: 1988, 1989, and 1990.

More than four-fifths of the wines from the Mâconnais are white.

There is a village named Chardonnay in the Mâconnais area, where it is said the grape's name originated.

Pouilly-Fuissé prices in many years have ended up higher than some of the great wines of Puligny-Montrachet and Meursault.

In an average year, around 450,000 cases of Pouilly-Fuissé are produced—not nearly enough to supply all of the restaurants and retail shops for worldwide consumption.

CÔTE CHÂLONNAISE

The Côte Châlonnaise is the least known of the major wine districts of Burgundy. Although the Châlonnaise is best known for such red wines as Givry and Mercurey (see the chapter on the red wines of Burgundy), it *does* produce some very good white wines that not many people know about, which means value for you. I'm referring to the wines of Montagny and Rully. These wines are of the highest quality produced in the area, similar to the white wines of the Côte d'Or.

MÂCONNAIS

The southernmost white-wine-producing area in Burgundy, the Mâconnais has a climate warmer than that of the Côte d'Or and Chablis. Mâcon wines, in general, are pleasant, light, uncomplicated, reliable table wines, which represent a very good value.

What are the quality levels of Mâconnais wines?

From basic to best:

Mâcon Blanc

Mâcon Supérieur

Mâcon-Villages

St-Véran

Pouilly-Vinzelles

Pouilly-Fuissé

Of all Mâcon wines, Pouilly-Fuissé is unquestionably one of the most popular. It is among the highest-quality Mâconnais wines, fashionable to drink in the United States long before most Americans discovered the splendors of wine. As wine consumption increased in America, Pouilly-Fuissé and other famous areas such as Pommard, Nuits-St-Georges, and Chablis became synonymous with the best wines of France, and could always be found on any restaurant's wine list.

In my opinion, Mâcon-Villages is the best value. Why pay more for Pouilly-Fuissé—sometimes three times as much—when a simple Mâcon will do just as nicely?

Best Bet of Recent Vintages of Mâcon White
1992

"If you start talking to him about 'Pooly-Foossy,' I'll walk right out."

OVERVIEW

Now that you're familiar with the many different white wines of Burgundy:

How do you choose the right one for you?

First look for the vintage year. With Burgundy, it's especially important to buy a good year. After that, your choice becomes a matter of taste and cost. If price is no object, aren't you lucky?

Decide if you prefer a light or a full-bodied wine. Also, after some trial and error, you may find that you prefer the wines of one shipper over another. Here are some of the shippers to look for when buying white Burgundy:

Bouchard Père & Fils
Joseph Drouhin
Louis Jadot
Louis Latour
Ropiteau Frères
Mommessin
Prosper Maufoux
Labouré-Roi
Chartron et Trebuchet
Olivier Leflaive Frères

Although 80 percent of Burgundy wines are sold through shippers, some fine estate-bottled wines are available in limited quantities in the United States. Some of the better ones are:

Domaine Leflaive (Meursault, Puligny-Montrachet)
Domaine Bachelet-Ramonet (Chassagne-Montrachet)
Domaine Bonneau du Martray (Corton-Charlemagne)
Domaine Matrot (Meursault)
Domaine Étienne Sauzet (Chassagne-Montrachet, Puligny-Montrachet)
Domaine Boillot (Meursault)
Domaine des Comtes Lafon (Meursault)

What are the trends in white Burgundy wines over the last ten years?

If anything, white Burgundy wines have gotten better over the last ten years. With the great vintages in 1988-90, and again in 1992, they continue to be high-priced but, for great Chardonnays, they're still worth it (with the exception of Chablis, which may be too pricey for the U.S. market). Mâcon wines remain one of today's great values in the world of wine, being made from 100% Chardonnay grapes, yet usually priced under $10 a bottle.

One of the most interesting things I have seen on the labels of French wines in the U.S. market, particularly from the Mâconnais, is the inclusion of the grape variety. French winemakers have finally realized that Americans have learned to buy wines by grape varieties.

I have also found that the major shippers have continued to make high-quality wines. Years ago there were quality problems with shippers' wines, but today they're some of the best.

Domaine Leflaive's wines are named for characters and places in a local medieval tale. The Chevalier of Puligny-Montrachet, lonely for his son who was off fighting in the Crusades, amused himself in the ravinelike vineyards (Les Combettes) with a local maiden (Pucelle), only to welcome the arrival of another son (Bâtard-Montrachet) nine months later.

Estate-bottled wines: The wine is made, produced, and bottled by the owner of the vineyards.

WiNE ANd food

When you choose a white Burgundy wine, you have a whole gamut of wonderful food possibilities. Let's say that you decide upon a wine from the Mâconnais area. Very reasonably priced, Mâconnais wines are suitable for picnics, as well as for more formal dinners. Or, you might select one of the fuller-bodied Côte de Beaune wines that can even stand up to a hearty steak, or if you prefer, an all-purpose wine, Chablis. Here are some tempting combinations offered by the winemakers.

Christian Moreau—A basic village Chablis is good as an apéritif and with hôrs d'oeuvres and salads. A great premier cru or grand cru Chablis needs something more special, such as lobster. It's an especially beautiful match if the wine has a few years' age on it.

André Gagey (Louis Jadot)—Says that Chablis is a great match for oysters, snails, and shellfish, but a "Grand Cru Chablis should be had with trout."

On white wines of the Côte de Beaune, Mr. Gagey gets a bit more specific. "With Village wines, which should be had at the beginning of the meal, try a light fish or quenelles (light dumplings)."

"Premier Cru and Grand Cru wines can stand up to heavier fish and shellfish such as lobster—but with a wine such as Corton-Charlemagne, smoked Scottish salmon is a tasty choice."

Mr. Gagey's parting words on the subject: "Never with meat."

Jean-François Bouchard—Enjoys Chablis as an apéritif or with such first courses as raw clams and oysters or charcuterie; it's nice with slightly spicy dishes, seafood salads and scallops Parisian or Provençal style.

Louis Latour—Believes that one should have Chablis with oysters and fish. Unlike most of the other experts in the trade, Mr. Latour says that the white wines of Burgundy go well with meat because of the wine's body. His recommendation for Corton-Charlemagne: "Have it in the middle of the afternoon with *foie gras.*"

Robert Drouhin—Has Chablis with any fish—seafood, oysters—but, "No cream sauce, please."

Côte de Beaune wines go well with "any fish except oysters, but without a heavy sauce." Some of the dishes Mr. Drouhin enjoys with these wines are "a richer fish, sweetbreads, veal—but not red meat."

> If you're taking a client out on a limited expense account, a safe wine to order is a Mâcon. If the sky's the limit, go for the Meursault!

For further reading on Burgundy wines, I recommend *Burgundy,* by Anthony Hanson, *Burgundy,* by Robert M. Parker, Jr., *Making Sense of Burgundy,* by Matt Kramer, and *The Great Domaines of Burgundy,* by Remington Norman.

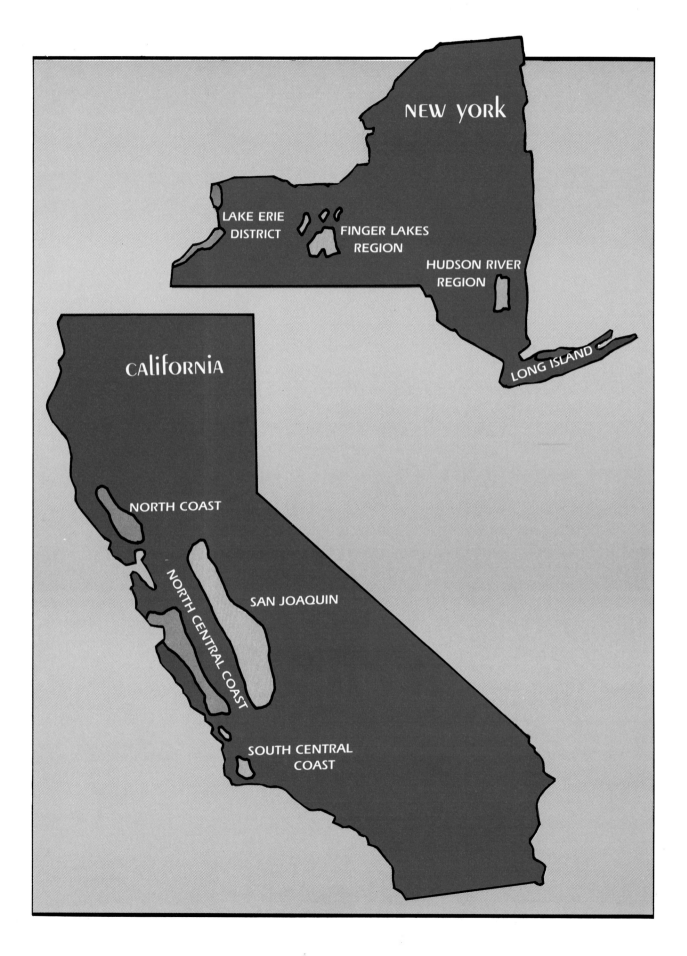

THE WHITE WINES of cAlifORNIA aNd NEW YORk

Before discussing the wines of California and New York, let's take a look at American drinking habits. You may wonder why it took so long for wine to become popular in the United States. You only have to look at the largest-selling beverage in the United States in 1960—milk! In 1960, Americans consumed less than one gallon of wine per person each year—quite a difference from 38 gallons of milk per year.

In 1990, just 30 years later, the leading beverage was soft drinks, with the typical American consuming an average of 50 gallons per year. Beer was in second place, while milk had fallen to third place. Wine consumption had doubled, to a still-modest two gallons per person.

Wine has never been a part of American culture. The average American consumes very little wine compared to the average European. Perhaps as America produces and imports better wines, we can expect to see a modest increase in the per capita consumption of these wines.

In the previous chapter, we discussed the white wines of France and the *appellation côntrolée* system. In the United States, we are beginning to develop a more systematic understanding of which viticultural regions exist in the main areas of winegrowing. So what you could describe as a U.S. appellation system is something called A.V.A., which stands for "American Viticultural Area."

Vintners are discovering, as their European counterparts did years ago, which grapes grow best in which particular soils and climatic conditions. To date, there are 124 viticultural areas in the United States. I believe the A.V.A. concept will become increasingly important to wine buying, as individual A.V.A.'s become known for certain grape varieties or wine styles.

For example, let's look at Napa Valley, in which Carneros is a good example of an A.V.A. It's the coolest climate in the Napa Valley, and since Chardonnay and Pinot Noir grapes need a cooler growing season to mature properly, these grapes are especially appropriate to that A.V.A.

Wine has never been America's favorite beverage. In fact, 40% of all Americans don't drink alcoholic beverages of any kind, and another 30% don't drink wine. This leaves only 30% of Americans who drink wine at all. In the final analysis, 5% of the population drinks 75% of all the wine.

The World's Top 10 Wine-Drinking Countries

Rank	Country	Gallons per Person
1	France	18
2	Italy	16
3	Portugal	16
4	Luxembourg	16
5	Argentina	14.5
6	Switzerland	12.5
7	Spain	11
8	Austria	9
9	Greece	8.5
10	Hungary	8

Source: California Wine Institute.

In the United States, a "wine drinker" is a person who drinks one glass of wine each week.

Before turning to the exciting world of California wines, I'd like to talk about the other major winemaking regions in the United States—New York State and the Pacific Northwest.

NEW YORK STATE

New York State is the second-largest wine-producing state in America. While New York produces less than one-tenth of California's volume, its wine production is 8 times greater than that of Washington State, another major producer of quality wines.

The four major wine regions in New York are:

Finger Lakes—with the largest wine production east of California

Hudson River Region—with a great concentration of premium farm wineries.

Lake Erie District—the largest grape-growing district east of California.

Long Island—New York's fastest-growing wine region

The Beginning of Winemaking in the United States

When colonists came to America, many of them settled in New England. They were very pleased to find vines already growing wild, so they didn't have to worry about importing their own.

The first thing they did was to prune the existing vines and to plant more of the same. Three years later—the time it takes before a mature grape crop can produce wine—they harvested the grapes and made the wine. After they tasted the first vintage, they were disappointed that the wine didn't taste the same as the wine they had drunk in Europe.

The only way to make their own style of wine was to bring their own grapes—actually, cuttings of the vines. Once again, ships from Europe landed on the East Coast and the colonists planted *Vitis vinifera* vines.

What happened? Nothing. The vines didn't grow. The cold was blamed, but actually the European vines lacked immunity to local plant diseases and pests. (If the colonists had had access to today's methods to control these problems, the *V. vinifera* grapes would have thrived on the East Coast, just as they do today.)

46

Which grapes grow in New York State?

There are three main categories:

Native American (*Vitis labrusca*)

French-American (hybrids)

European (*Vitis vinifera*)

NATIVE AMERICAN VARIETIES

The *Vitis labrusca,* or Native American, varieties are very popular among grape-growers in New York State because they are hardy grapes that can withstand cold winters. Among the most familiar grapes of the *Vitis labrusca* family are Concord, Catawba, and Delaware. Traditionally, until the last decade, these were the grapes that were used to make most New York State wines. In describing these wines, the words "foxy," "grapey," "Welch's," and "Manischewitz" are often used. These words are a sure sign of *V. labrusca.*

EUROPEAN VARIETIES

Thirty years ago, some New York wineries began to experiment with the traditional European (*Vitis vinifera*) grapes. Dr. Konstantin Frank, a Russian viticulturist skilled in cold-climate grape-growing, came to the United States and catalyzed efforts to grow *Vitis vinifera* in New York. This was unheard of—and laughed at—years ago. Other vintners predicted that he'd fail, that it was impossible to grow *vinifera* in New York's cold and capricious climate.

"What do you mean?" Dr. Frank replied. "I'm from Russia—it's even colder there."

Most people still laughed, but Charles Fournier of Gold Seal Vineyards was intrigued enough to give Konstantin Frank a chance to prove his theory.

Sure enough, Dr. Frank was successful with the *vinifera* and has produced some world-class wines, especially his Riesling and Chardonnay. So have many other New York wineries, thanks to the vision and courage of Dr. Frank and Charles Fournier.

The average American consumes about one-tenth the amount of wine that the average French or Italian person drinks.

DRY

Dr. Konstantin Frank

Johannisberg Riesling

NEW YORK FINGER LAKES.
ESTATE BOTTLED AND GROWN BY
KONSTANTIN D. FRANK & SONS VINIFERA WINE CELLARS, LTD.
HAMMONDSPORT, N.Y. 14840. ALCOHOL 10.5% BY VOLUME.
CONTAINS SULFITES

FRENCH-AMERICAN VARIETIES

In an effort to hedge their bets, some New York winemakers have compromised by planting French-American hybrid varieties. These combine European taste characteristics with American vine hardiness to withstand New York's cold winters. These varieties were originally developed by French viticulturists in the nineteenth century. Seyval Blanc and Vidal are the most promising white wine varieties; Baco Noir and Chancellor are the best reds.

What have been the trends in New York wines over the last ten years?

The most significant developments have been in the wines of Long Island, which saw the largest growth of new wineries. The predominant use of *vinifera* varieties allows Long Island wineries to compete more effectively in the world market, and Long Island's longer growing season offers more potential for red grapes.

The Hudson Valley has seen the addition of a major winery, called Millbrook, which has shown that this region can produce world-class wines—not only white, but red, from such grapes as Merlot and Cabernet Franc.

The wines of the Finger Lakes region continue to get better as the winemakers work with grapes that thrive in the cooler climate, including European varieties such as Riesling, Chardonnay and Pinot Noir.

Hargrave Vineyard
North Fork
Long Island   New York

Chardonnay

Long Island has seen the fastest growth of new vineyards. In the last ten years, its grape-growing acreage has increased from 100 acres to more than 1,000 acres, with more expansion expected in the future.

Today, more than 80 New York State wineries produce vinifera wines.

Wineries to look for in New York State are:
The Finger Lakes—Dr. Konstantin Frank, Glenora, Herman Weimer, Wagner
The Hudson Valley—Millbrook
Long Island—Lenz, Hargrave, Pindar Palmer, Christina

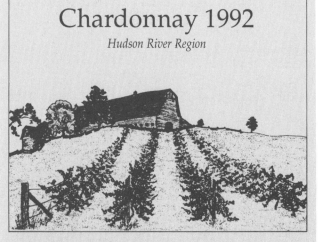

MILLBROOK®

Chardonnay 1992
Hudson River Region

PRODUCED AND BOTTLED BY   750 Ml
©1991 MILLBROOK WINERY, INC   12% ALC. BY VOL.
MILLBROOK, N.Y. 12545   CONTAINS SULFITES

THE pacific NORTHWEST

WASHINGTON STATE

In Washington, the climatic conditions are a little cooler than in California, and the winegrowing regions are protected from Washington's famous rains by the Cascade Mountains. The two major white grapes are Chardonnay and Riesling,. Sémillon and Sauvignon Blanc are grown there as well.

There are three major A.V.A.'s: Columbia Valley, Yakima, and Walla Walla. Some of the wineries to look for include Columbia Winery, Hogue Cellars, Leonetti Cellars, Woodward Canyon Winery, and the largest winery, Château Ste. Michelle (which is the largest producer of Riesling wine in the United States).

Cabernet Sauvignon and Merlot grow well in Washington State's Columbia Valley, which is on the same latitude as Bordeaux, France.

OREGON

Oregon, because of its climate, is becoming well known for Burgundian-style wines. By Burgundian style I'm referring to Chardonnay and Pinot Noir, which are the major grapes planted in Oregon. The major A.V.A. in Oregon is the Willamette Valley, near Portland. Other A.V.A's include Rogue Valley and Umpqua.

Wineries to look for include Adelsheim, Eyrie Vineyards, Knudsen Erath, Ponzi Vineyards, Rex Hill, Sokol Blosser, and Tualatin. Also, the famous Burgundy producer Joseph Drouhin now owns a winery in Oregon called Domain Drouhin, producing, not surprisingly, Burgundy-style wines.

Of course, very good wines are produced throughout the United States, in such places as Idaho, Michigan, and Texas, but a discussion of each is beyond the scope of this book. For further reading, I recommend *The Wines of America,* by Leon D. Adams, and *American Wine,* by Anthony Dias Blue.

BARREL FERMENTED

Chateau Ste Michelle

COLUMBIA VALLEY

CHARDONNAY

1 9 9 3

PRODUCED AND BOTTLED BY CHATEAU STE. MICHELLE
WOODINVILLE, WA · USA · ALC. 13.0% BY VOL.

Gallo sells one out of every four bottles of American wine. They produce more than 62 million cases per year—more than a million cases per week.

The best-known wineries of California in the 1950s:
Wente
Martini
Inglenook
Beaulieu
Korbel
Concannon
Beringer
Krug
Paul Masson
Almaden

CAliforNiA

What are the main viticultural areas of California?

The map at the beginning of the chapter should help familiarize you with the winemaking regions. It's easier to remember them if you divide them into four groups:

North Coast— Napa County
Sonoma County
Mendocino County
Lake County

North Central Coast— Monterey County
Santa Clara County
Livermore

South Central Coast— San Luis Obispo County
Santa Barbara County

San Joaquin Valley— Central Valley

Although you may be most familiar with the names Napa and Sonoma, the fact is that only 12 percent of all California wine comes from these two regions combined. In fact, the bulk of California wine is from the San Joaquin Valley, where mostly "jug" wines are produced. This region accounts for 54 percent of the wine grapes planted. Maybe that doesn't seem too exciting—that the production of jug wine dominates the California winemaking industry—but Americans are not atypical in this respect. In France, for example, the A.O.C. (Appellation d'Origine Contrôlée) wines account for only 35 percent of all French wines, while the rest are everyday table wines.

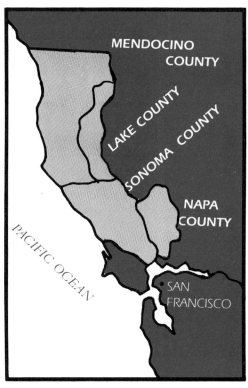

Traditionally, the areas known for producing fine varietal wines in California are the counties along the North Coast: Napa, Sonoma, Mendocino, and Lake.

A Note on Jug Wines

The phrase "jug wine" refers to simple, uncomplicated, everyday drinking wine. You're probably familiar with these types of wine: they're usually labeled with a generic name, such as "Chablis" or "Burgundy." Inexpensive and well made, these wines were originally bottled in jugs, rather than in conventional wine bottles, hence the name "jug wine." They are very popular and account for the largest volume of California wine sold in the United States.

Ernest & Julio Gallo is the major producer of jug wines in California. In fact, many people credit the Gallo brothers with converting American drinking habits from spirits to wine. Several other wineries also produce jug wines, among them, Almaden, Paul Masson, and Taylor California Cellars.

In my opinion, the best-made jug wines in the world are from California. They maintain both consistency and quality from year to year.

One of the reasons California produces such a wide variety of wine is that is has so many different climates. Some areas are as cool as Burgundy, Champagne, and the Rhine, while others are as warm as the Rhône Valley, Italy, Spain, and Portugal. If that's not diverse enough, these winegrowing areas have inner districts with "microclimates," or climates-within-climates. One of the microclimates (which are among the designated A.V.A.'s) in Sonoma County, for example, is the Alexander Valley; Dry Creek in Sonoma and Stag's Leap in Napa are two others that appear on wine labels.

To better understand this concept, let's take a close look at the Château St. Jean label.

State:
California

County:
Sonoma

Viticultural Area:
Alexander Valley

Vineyard:
Robert Young

Winery:
Château St. Jean

Chardonnay grapes are very expensive, with a top price of $2,000 per ton.

California wineries attract 2.5 million visitors each year.

Acres of wine grapes planted in Napa: 36,360
Number of wineries: 219

Acres of wine grapes planted in Sonoma: 34,392
Number of wineries: 166

Acres of wine grapes planted in Mendocino: 12,421
Number of wineries: 42

Is there any Chardonnay in a California Chablis?

Probably not, since Chardonnay is the most expensive grape used to make some of the best-quality wines in California (that's *one* reason to remember the varietal name "Chardonnay").

"Why," you ask, "did you say, in the last chapter, that Chablis must have 100 percent Chardonnay?"

Good question! In France the standards set by the Appellation d'Origine Contrôlée (A.O.C.) regulations require this percentage. Early California winemakers, however, "borrowed" the names of famous European winemaking regions, such as Chablis, and applied them to their own wines, regardless of the grape variety used to produce them.

What's California's winemaking history?

Although California wines have come into national and international prominence only recently—within the past thirty years—the winemaking industry in the state is more than 200 years old.

1769: Padre Junipero Serra came to California from Mexico with the V. vinifera grape to plant for his missions.

1831: Jean Louis Vignes brought the first European grape cuttings of classic wine varieties to California.

1861: Count Agoston Haraszthy brought 100,000 V. vinifera vine cuttings from Europe. The story goes that it was the governor of California who selected Haraszthy to go to Europe to buy the cuttings. Even at this early date, California saw the potential for a wine industry.

1899: California wines were winning medals in international competition by the late 1800s.

In 1861, Mrs. Lincoln served American wines in the White House.

When Robert Louis Stevenson honeymooned in the Napa Valley in 1880, he described the efforts of local vintners to match soil and climate with the best possible varietals: "One corner of land after another . . . this is a failure; that is better; this is best. So bit by bit, they grope about for their Clos de Vougeot and Lafite . . . and the wine is bottled poetry."

The California Gold Rush of 1849 started a mass migration to the West Coast. While many were following the call, "Go west, young man," not so many were getting rich panning for gold. What did they do? The same thing any businessman would do to survive—change businesses.

Since the land was free and open, many chose farming as the most logical option, and one of the most popular crops was grapes. This led to the real beginning of the California wine industry.

Now, don't get the idea that frustrated gold miners created the whole California winemaking industry. In fact, many Europeans who settled in California brought their grapes and winemaking tradition with them.

In 1919 something terrible happened, at least for the wine industry—Prohibition! Prohibition lasted for fourteen miserable years, until 1933.

What effect did Prohibition have on the California wine industry?

By the end of Prohibition, most wineries had gone out of business. The only wineries to survive legitimately were those that produced table grapes for home winemaking and, of course, for sacramental wine.

Beringer, Beaulieu, and the Christian Brothers are a few of the wineries that survived this dry time by supplying sacramental wine. Since these wineries didn't have to interrupt production during Prohibition, they had a jump on those that had to start all over again after the amendment was repealed. But once again, we're getting ahead of our story.

In 1920 there were more than 700 wineries in California. By the end of Prohibition there were 160.

In 1930, there were 188,000 acres of vineyards in California. Today, there are more than 326,000 acres.

One Way to Get Around Prohibition . . .

During Prohibition, people used to buy grape concentrate from California and have it shipped to the East Coast. The top of the container was stamped in big, bold letters: CAUTION: DO NOT ADD SUGAR OR YEAST OR ELSE FERMENTATION WILL TAKE PLACE!

Of course, we know the formula: Sugar + Yeast = Alcohol. Do you want to guess how many people had the sugar and yeast ready the very moment the concentrate arrived?

When did California begin to make better-quality wines?

As early as the 1940s, Frank Schoonmaker, an importer and writer, and one of the first American wine experts, convinced some California winery owners to market their best wines, using varietal labels.

Robert Mondavi may be one of the best examples of a winemaker who concentrated solely on varietal wine production. In 1966, Mondavi left the Charles Krug Winery and started the Robert Mondavi Winery. His role was important to the evolution of varietals in California. Although he wasn't the first, he was among the first major winemakers to make the switch and concentrate on the new venture.

A varietal wine is labelled with the predominant grape variety used in making the wine. Federal regulations as of 1983 specify that at least 75% of the grapes used must be of the variety cited.

Creative Financing—Overheard at "The Diner" in Yountville, Napa: "How do you make a small fortune in the wine business?" "Start with a large fortune and buy a winery."

How did California come so far so fast in the wine industry?

First and foremost, Americans became "wine conscious." Without that interest, there would have been no need to develop the product and no economic justification for its existence. And it is, of course, the American way to create a product and to go as far with it as possible: "We'll beat out the competition; we'll show that we're the best and can compete with the best."

Location—Napa and Sonoma, the two major quality-wine regions, are one-and-a-half hours from San Francisco by car. The proximity of these regions to the city encourages people to visit often, taste the wines, and participate—for business or pleasure, or both.

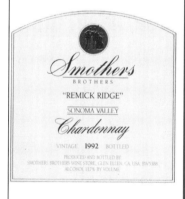

Weather—Plenty of sunshine, warm temperatures, and a long growing season all add up to good conditions for growing many varieties of grapes. California is certainly subject to sudden changes in weather—as is any other wine-growing region in the world—but a fickle climate is not a major worry to Californians.

Money and Marketing Strategy—This factor simply cannot be over-emphasized. Perhaps marketing does not *make* the wine, but it certainly helps *sell* it. Going back to 1967, when National Distillers bought Almaden, large corporations with tremendous resources and expertise in advertising and promotion entered the wine business and brought California wines to the attention of buyers around the world. Other corporate participants included Pillsbury, Coca-Cola, and even Otsuka Pharmaceutical Company of Japan.

The University of California at Davis, and Fresno State University—These schools have been the training grounds for many young California winemakers. They learn new techniques from a truly scientific study of wine: The soil, the different strains of yeast, temperature-controlled fermentation, and other winemaking and viticultural techniques.

From the Corporate Ladder to the Vine

The pioneers of the back-to-the-land movement:

"Farmer"	Winery	Profession
Robert Travers	Mayacamas	Investment banker
David Stare	Dry Creek	Civil engineer
Tom Jordan	Jordan	Geologist
Rodney Strong	Rodney Strong	Dancer/Choreographer
Jack Davies	Schramsberg	Management Consultant
James Barrett	Chateau Montelena	Attorney
Tom Burgess	Burgess	Air Force pilot
Eugene Trefethen	Trefethen	Industrialist
Brooks Firestone	Firestone	Take a guess!

How is California winemaking different from the European technique?

European winemaking has established traditions that have remained essentially unchanged for hundreds of years. These practices involve the ways in which grapes are grown and harvested, and in some cases include winemaking procedures.

In California, there are few traditions, and the winemakers are able to take full advantage of modern technology. Furthermore, there is freedom to experiment and to create new products. Some of the experimenting the California winemakers do, such as combining different grape varieties to make new styles of wine, is prohibited by some European wine-control

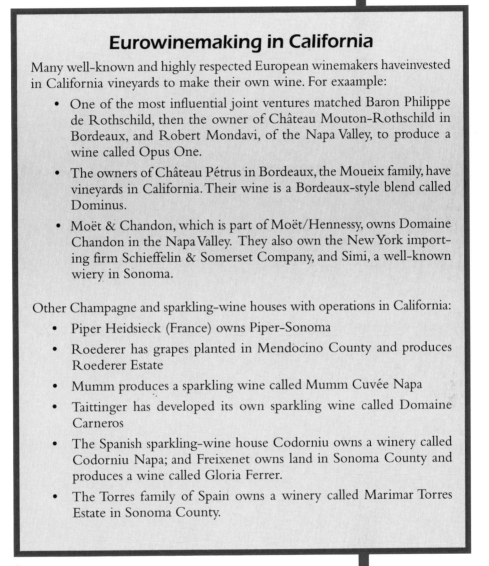

Eurowinemaking in California

Many well-known and highly respected European winemakers have invested in California vineyards to make their own wine. For exaample:

- One of the most influential joint ventures matched Baron Philippe de Rothschild, then the owner of Château Mouton-Rothschild in Bordeaux, and Robert Mondavi, of the Napa Valley, to produce a wine called Opus One.

- The owners of Château Pétrus in Bordeaux, the Moueix family, have vineyards in California. Their wine is a Bordeaux-style blend called Dominus.

- Moët & Chandon, which is part of Moët/Hennessy, owns Domaine Chandon in the Napa Valley. They also own the New York importing firm Schieffelin & Somerset Company, and Simi, a well-known wiery in Sonoma.

Other Champagne and sparkling-wine houses with operations in California:

- Piper Heidsieck (France) owns Piper-Sonoma

- Roederer has grapes planted in Mendocino County and produces Roederer Estate

- Mumm produces a sparkling wine called Mumm Cuvée Napa

- Taittinger has developed its own sparkling wine called Domaine Carneros

- The Spanish sparkling-wine house Codorniu owns a winery called Codorniu Napa; and Freixenet owns land in Sonoma County and produces a wine called Gloria Ferrer.

- The Torres family of Spain owns a winery called Marimar Torres Estate in Sonoma County.

laws. Californians thus have opportunities to try many new ideas—opportunities sometimes forbidden to European winemakers.

Another way in which California winemaking is different from European winemaking is that many Californians carry an entire line of wine. Many of the larger California wineries produce more than 20 different labels. In Bordeaux, most châteaus produce only one or two wines.

In addition to modern technology and experimentation, you can't ignore the fundamentals of winegrowing: California's rainfall, weather patterns, and soils are very different from those of Europe.

"Surprisingly good, isn't it? It's Gallo. Mort and I simply got tired of being snobs."

The Gallo "University"

The Ernest & Julio Gallo Winery celebrated its 60th year in the wine industry in 1993. The two brothers were in business long before California wines became popular in the United States and internationally. Not only is theirs the largest winery in the United States, but it also has a reputation for maintaining the highest standards in the production of its wines. Many of the famous winemakers of today's smaller California wineries learned their trade under the guidance of Ernest & Julio Gallo.

Here's a short list of some of Gallo's "graduates," and the wineries where they've worked:

Winemaker	Winery
Bill Bonetti	Sonoma Cutrer
Jerry Luper	Chateau Montelena, Chateau Bouchaine, Rutherford Hill
Dick Peterson	Monterey Vineyards
Philip Togni	Togni Vineyards
Walter Schug	Joseph Phelps
Leigh Knowles	Beaulieu Vineyards

THE WINE CELLARS OF

ERNEST & JULIO GALLO

ERNEST & JULIO GALLO VINTED & CELLARED THIS
WINE & BOTTLED IT IN MODESTO CALIF.
ALCOHOL 12.5% BY VOLUME

Why is California wine so confusing?

Many students ask me this, and I can only tell them that I'm glad I learned all about the wines of France, Italy, Germany, Spain, and the rest of Europe before I tackled California—because the European wines were so much easier to understand. There are many more details to learn about California wines than there are about any of the others. We've already covered most of the reasons that California wines are so confusing: There are more than 800 wineries in California, most of them making more than one wine; price differences are reflected in the styles (you can get a Chardonnay wine in any price range from $5 to $75—so how do you choose?); constant changes in the wine industry; experimentation, which keeps the California wine industry in a state of flux; and the labels, another source of mega-information.

"If it's a California wine you wish, Mr. Larry will assist you."

What about the prices of California varietal wines?

You can't necessarily equate quality with price. Some excellent varietal wines that are produced in California are well within the budget of the average consumer. On the other hand, some varietals (primarily Chardonnay and Cabernet Sauvignon) may be quite expensive.

As in any market, it is mainly supply-and-demand that determines price. However, new wineries are affected by start-up costs, which sometimes are reflected in the price of the wine. Older, established wineries, which had long ago amortized their investments, are able to keep their prices low when the supply/demand ratio calls for it.

Remember, when you're buying California wine, price doesn't always reflect quality.

California wine has no classification system that resembles the European equivalent.

So you want to buy a vineyard in California? Today, one acre in the Napa Valley costs $30,000 to $40,000 unplanted, and it takes an additional $6,000 per acre to plant. This per-acre investment sees no return for three to five years. To this, add the cost of building the winery, buying the equipment, and hiring the winemaker.

As one California winemaker said: "We release no wine before the bank tells us that it's ready."

I've mentioned stainless-steel fermentation tanks so often by now that I'll give you a definition, in case you need one. These tanks are temperature controlled: They allow the winemaker to control the temperature at which the wine ferments. For example, a winemaker could ferment wines at a low temperature to retain their fruitiness and delicacy, while preventing browning and oxidation.

Ambassador Zellerbach, who created Hanzell Winery, was one of the first California winemakers to use small French oak aging barrels because he wanted to recreate a Burgundian style.

"A winemaker's task is to bring to perfection the natural potential that is in the fruit itself."—Warren Winiarski, winemaker/owner, Stag's Leap Wine Cellars, Napa Valley.

Another note on winemakers and style: In California many winemakers move around from one winery to another just as a good chef may move from one restaurant to the next. This is not uncommon. They may choose to carry and use the same "recipe" from place to place, if it is particularly successful, and sometimes they will experiment and create new styles.

What's meant by "style"? How are different styles of wine actually created?

Style refers to the characteristics of the grapes and wine. It is the trademark of the individual winemaker—an "artist" who tries different techniques to explore the fullest potential of the grapes.

Most winemakers will tell you that 95 percent of winemaking is in the quality of the grapes they begin with. The other 5 percent can be traced to the "personal touch" of the winemaker. Here are just a few of the hundreds of decisions a winemaker must make when developing his style of wine:

When should the grapes be harvested?

Should the juice be fermented in stainless-steel tanks or oak barrels? How long should it be fermented? At what temperature?

Should the wine be aged at all? How long? If so, should it be aged in oak? What kind of oak—American, French?

What varieties of grape should be blended, and in what proportion?

How long should the wine be aged in the bottle before it is sold?

The list goes on. Because there are so many variables in wine making, producers can create many styles of wine from the same grape variety—so you can choose the style that suits *your* taste.

The point of all this is that California, unlike Europe, is still looking for its own style, and because of the relative freedom of winemaking in the United States, the "style" of California may continue to be *diversity*.

How do I choose a good California wine?

One way is to look at the label. California labels tell you everything you need to know about the wine—and more. Here are some quick tips you can use when you scan the shelves at your favorite retailer. The label shown below will serve as an example.

The most important piece of information on the label is the producer's name. In this case, the producer is Beringer.

As of January 1983, if the grape variety is on the label, a minimum of 75 percent of the wine must be derived from that grape variety. If the wine was made before 1983, it must contain at least 51 percent of the labelled variety. The label shows that the wine is made from the Sauvignon Blanc grape.

If the wine bears a vintage date, 95 percent of the grapes must have been harvested that year.

If the wine is designated "California," then 100 percent of the grapes must have been grown in California.

If the label designates a certain federally recognized viticultural area (A.V.A.), such as Napa Valley (as on our sample label), then at least 85 percent of the grapes used to make that wine must have been grown in that location.

The alcohol content is given in percentages. Usually, the higher the percentage of alcohol, the "fuller" the wine will be.

"Produced and bottled by" means that at least 75 percent of the wine was fermented by the winery named on the label.

Some wineries will tell you the exact varietal content of the wine, and/or the sugar content of the grapes when they were picked, and/or the amount of residual sugar (to let you know how sweet or dry the wine is).

Why do some Chardonnays and Cabernet Sauvignons cost more than other varietals?

In addition to everything we've mentioned before, many wineries age these wines in wood—sometimes for more than a year. Oak barrels have doubled in price over the last five years, averaging $550 per barrel. Add to this the cost of the grapes and the length of time before the wine is actually sold.

What are the white-grape varieties grown in California?

One of them is Chardonnay, sometimes labelled Pinot Chardonnay. This green-skinned European (*V. vinifera*) grape is considered the finest white-grape variety in the world. It is responsible for all the great French white Burgundies such as Meursault, Chablis, and Puligny-Montrachet. In California, it has been the most successful white grape, yielding a wine of tremendous character and magnificent flavor. The wines are often aged

There are 70 A.V.A.'s in California. Some of the best known are:
Napa Valley
Sonoma Valley
Russian River Valley
Alexander Valley
Dry Creek Valley
Los Caneros
Anderson Valley
Santa Cruz Mountain
Livermore Valley
Paso Robles
Edna Valley
Fiddletown

The legal limits for the alcohol content of table wine are 7% to 13.9%, with a 1.5% allowance either way, so long as the allowance doesn't go beyond the legal limits. If the alcohol content of a table wine exceeds 14%, the label must show that. Sparkling wines may be 10% to 13.9%, with the 1.5% allowance. Appetizer wines: 17% to 20%; dessert wines: 18% to 20%. There is a 1% allowance for these last two types of wine.

If an individual vineyard is noted on the bottle, 95% of the grapes must have come from the named vineyard, which must be located within a federally approved A.V.A.

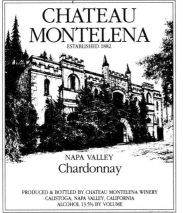

CHATEAU MONTELENA
ESTABLISHED 1882

NAPA VALLEY
Chardonnay

PRODUCED & BOTTLED BY CHATEAU MONTELENA WINERY
CALISTOGA, NAPA VALLEY, CALIFORNIA
ALCOHOL 13.5% BY VOLUME

ESTATE BOTTLED
1992
SONOMA CUTRER
RUSSIAN RIVER RANCHES

SONOMA COAST CHARDONNAY BOTTLED BY SONOMA-CUTRER, WINDSOR, CA. TABLE WINE

More than 300 different California wineries market Chardonnay.

The leading white table wines produced in the United States in 1994:
1. Chardonnay
2. Sauvignon Blanc/Fumé Blanc
3. Chenin Blanc

in small oak barrels, increasing the wines' complexity. In the vineyard, yields are fairly low and the grapes command high prices. Chardonnay is always dry, and benefits from aging more than any other American white wine. Superior examples can keep and develop well in the bottle for five years or longer.

What makes one Chardonnay different from another?

Put it this way: There are many brands of ice cream on the market. They use similar ingredients, but there is only one Ben & Jerry's. The same is true for wine. Among the many things to consider: Is a wine aged in wood or stainless steel? How long does it remain in the barrel (part of the style of the winemaker)? Where do the grapes come from?

Best Bets for California Chardonnay
1990   1991   1992   1993

So far California has been blessed with great vintages in the 1990's.

Why is Sauvignon Blanc often labelled as Fumé Blanc? Robert Mondavi found that no one was buying Sauvignon Blanc, so he changed its name to Fumé Blanc. Strictly a marketing maneuver—it was still the same wine. Result: Sales took off. The only mistake Mondavi made was not trademarking the name, so now anyone can use it (and many producers do).

What are the other major California white-wine grapes?

Sauvignon Blanc—sometimes labelled Fumé Blanc. This is one of the grapes used in making the dry white wines of the Graves region of Bordeaux, and the white wines of Sancerre and Pouilly-Fumé in the Loire Valley of France. This grape is capable of producing as good a wine in California as it does in France. It is sometimes aged in small oak barrels and occasionally blended with the Sémillon Blanc.

STERLING VINEYARDS

ESTATE BOTTLED

Sauvignon Blanc

NAPA VALLEY

GROWN, PRODUCED AND BOTTLED BY
STERLING VINEYARDS
CALISTOGA, NAPA VALLEY, CALIF. ALCOHOL 13% BY VOLUME

Napa Valley
FUMÉ BLANC
Dry Sauvignon Blanc
ALCOHOL 13% BY VOLUME
PRODUCED AND BOTTLED BY
ROBERT MONDAVI WINERY
OAKVILLE, CALIFORNIA

Johannisberg Riesling—The true Riesling responsible for the best German wines of the Rhein and Mosel—and the Alsace wines of France—is also called White Riesling, or just Riesling. This grape produces white wine of distinctive varietal character in every style from bone-dry to very sweet dessert wines, which are often much better by themselves than with dessert. The nose of White Riesling at its finest is always lively, fragrant, and both fruity and flowery.

In 1981, the BATF requested that the Wine Institute propose industry-wide standard definitions for the terms "Late Harvest" and other similar designations that link wine style to picking time. The categories proposed with their associated grape-sugar levels at harvest generally follow the terms established by the German Wine Law of 1971 (see page 65):

Early Harvest—Equivalent to a German Kabinett, this term refers to wine made from grapes picked at a *maximum* of 20° Brix.

Regular or Normal—No specific label designation will be used to connote wines made from fruit of traditional maturity levels, 20°–24° Brix.

Late Harvest—This term is equivalent to a German Auslese and requires a *minimum* sugar level of 24° Brix at harvest.

Select Late Harvest—Equivalent to a German Beerenauslese, the sugar-level *minimum* is 28° Brix.

Special Select Late Harvest—This, the highest maturity-level designation, requires that the grapes be picked at a minimum sugar content of 35° Brix, the same level necessary for a German Trockenbeerenauslese.

California Ingenuity

Several wineries in California started to market their Late Harvest Riesling with German names such as Trockenbeerenauslese. The German government complained, and this practice was discontinued. One winemaker, though, began marketing his wine as T.B.A., the abbreviation for Trockenbeerenauslese. Again there was a complaint. This time the winemaker argued his case, saying that T.B.A. was not an abbreviation for Trockenbeerenauslese, but for *Totally Botrytis Affected*. Stay tuned for more.

1976—Château Montelena Chardonnay won first place in Paris in a blind tasting with French white Burgundies. At the same tasting, Stag's Leap Cabernet Sauvignon placed above the top French Bordeaux.

Robert Mondavi was a great promoter for the California wine industry. "He was able to prove to the public what the people within the industry already knew—that California could produce world-class wines," said Eric Wente.

Chenin Blanc—This is one of the most widely planted grapes in the Loire Valley. In California, the grape yields a very attractive, soft, light-bodied wine. It is usually made very dry or semi-sweet; it is a perfect apéritif wine, simple and fruity.

Gewürztraminer—This grape is commonly grown both in Germany and in Alsace, France. The wine is often finished in a slightly sweet to medium-sweet style to counter the grape's tendency towards bitterness, but dry versions have also shown quite well.

What are the trends in the wines of California over the last ten years?

Ten years ago we were asking if California wines were entitled to be compared with European wines. Now, California wines are available worldwide—shipments for exports have increased dramatically over recent years to places such as Japan, Germany, and England. Today, you can find California wines in great French restaurants. There is a worldwide acceptance of California wines.

There has been a trend towards wineries specializing in particular grape varieties. Ten years ago, I would have talked about which are the best wineries in California. Today, I'm more likely to talk about which winery makes the best Chardonnay, which winery makes the best Sauvignon Blanc, and the same would hold true for the reds, narrowing it down to who makes the best Cabernet, Pinot Noir, or Merlot.

An era of great experimentation with winemaking techniques is over, and now the winemakers are just making the finest possible wines they can from what they've learned in the '80s. I do expect to see some further experimentation in determining which grape varieties grow best in the various A.V.A.'s and microclimates. The wineries have also become more food-conscious in winemaking, adjusting their wine styles to go better with various kinds of food.

Chardonnay and Cabernet Sauvignon remain the two major grape varieties, but my projection is that there will be much more Merlot planted in California. Sauvignon Blanc (also called Fumé Blanc) wines have gotten better. They're easier to consume when young, although they still don't have the cachet of a Chardonnay. However, other white-grape varieties, such as Riesling and Chenin Blanc, aren't meeting with the same success, and they're harder to sell today. Still, just to keep it interesting, some winemakers are introducing some additional European varietals to the California wine scene, including Italy's Sangiovese, and Grenache and Viognier from France.

American wine drinkers are moving away from *generic* towards *varietal*. Ten years ago, diners would come into Windows on the World and ask for a glass of Chablis. Today, they not only ask for Chardonnay, but they'll ask, "Which Chardonnay do you have today?" California has been very successful in creating affordable varietal wines. At the same time, even Gallo, which was known for its generic wines, has come out with a $30 bottle of Chardonnay and a $60 bottle of Cabernet Sauvignon. Critics have raved about the quality of the wine.

California still produces 90 percent of the wine made in the United

States. Significantly, California hasn't lost any market share. Still, the creation of new wineries is slowing down. Also, many of the corporate players are no longer in the game. For example, Coca-Cola realized it could make more money selling soft drinks, so it abandoned the wine business.

Finally, one must not forget the impact of the plant louse phylloxera, which has been killing the vines of California for the past few years. It's difficult to predict how much of an effect it will have in the coming years on the growing of grapes and on the prices of California wines. It will require large scale replanting of many California vineyards, which many predict could lead to improvement in vineyard management techniques and, ultimately, in wine quality.

WiNE ANd food

Margrit Biever and Robert Mondavi (Robert Mondavi Winery)— With Chardonnay: oysters, lobster, a more complex fish with sauce *beurre blanc*, pheasant salad with truffles. With Sauvignon Blanc: traditional white meat or fish course, sautéed or grilled fish (as long as it isn't an oily fish).

Francis Mahoney (Carneros Creek Winery)—With Chardonnay: fowl, ham, and seafood in sauces. With Sauvignon Blanc: fish, turkey, shellfish, and appetizers.

Katie Wetzel-Murphy (Alexander Valley Vineyards)—With Chardonnay: salmon with lemon or cream sauce, a light veal dish with mushrooms. With Riesling: chicken breasts poached with raspberry vinaigrette, cream of chanterelle soup.

Sam J. Sebastiani (Viansa Winery)—With Chardonnay: grilled baby salmon with shallots and fresh dill sauce. With Riesling: Brie tart with sliced green apples and Riesling glaze. With Sauvignon Blanc: rye toast triangles with fresh oysters and pesto.

David Stare (Dry Creek)—With Chardonnay: poached salmon with *beurre blanc*. With Sauvignon Blanc: simply prepared poultry and fish— except barbecued salmon.

Warren Winiarski (Stag's Leap Wine Cellars)—With Chardonnay: seviche, shellfish, salmon with a light hollandaise sauce.

Janet Trefethen (Trefethen Vineyards)—With Chardonnay: barbecued whole salmon in a sorrel sauce. With White Riesling: sautéed bay scallops with julienne vegetables.

For further reading on California wines I reccommend A Wine Atlas of California, by Bob Thompson, Wines of California, by James Halliday, and Making Sense of California Wine, by Matt Kramer. Lovers of gossip should have fun reading Napa, by James Conaway.

California wineries included in the 1993 Wine Spectator Critics' Choice Selections of the Best Wineries in the World:
Arrowood
Beaulieu
Beringer
Bonny Doon
Buena Vista
Caymus
Chalone
Chateau St. Jean
Clos du Bois
Codorniu Napa
Cuvaison
Diamond Creek
Domaine Carneros
Domaine Chandon
Dominus
Duckhorn
Dunn
Far Niente
Ferrari-Carano
Flora Springs
Forman
Franciscan
E & J Gallo Estate
Grgich Hills
Heitz
Hess Collection
William Hill
Inglenook–Napa Valley
Iron Horse
Jordan
Kendall-Jackson
Kenwood
Kistler
Kunde
Laurel Glen
Maison Deutz
Markham
Matanzas Creek
Merryvale
Robert Mondavi
Monticello
Mumm Napa Valley
Nalle
Niebaum-Coppola
Joseph Phelps
Pine Ridge
Piper Sonoma
Ridge
Roederer Estate
Saintsbury
Scharffenberger
Schramsberg
Silverado
Simi
Sonoma-Cutrer
Spottswoode
Stag's Leap
Sterling
Rodney Strong

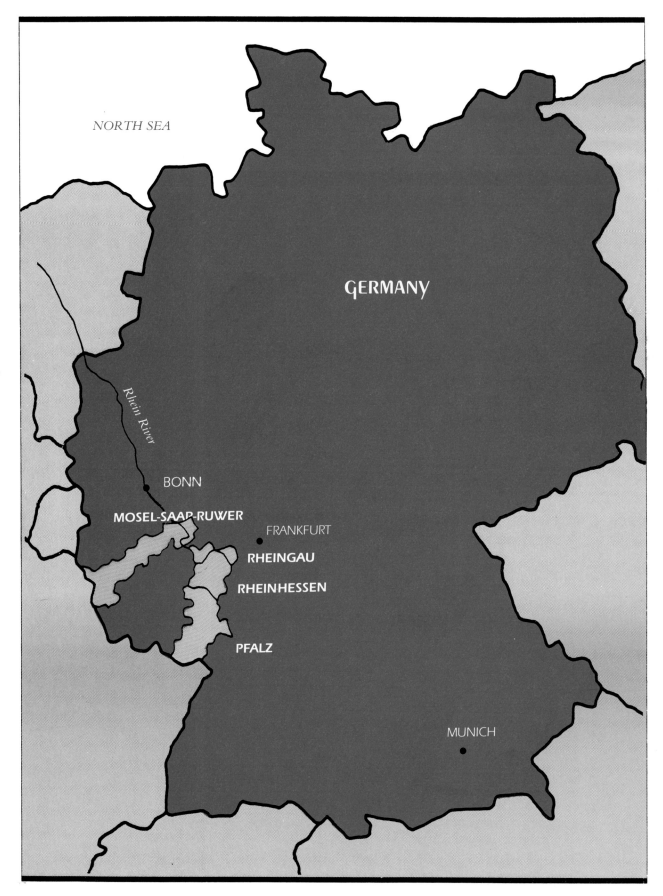

NORTH SEA

GERMANY

Rhein River

BONN

MOSEL-SAAR-RUWER

FRANKFURT

RHEINGAU

RHEINHESSEN

PFALZ

MUNICH

THE WHITE WINES of GERMANY

Before we begin our study of the white wines of Germany, tell me this: Have you memorized the seven Grand Crus of Chablis, the 32 Grand Crus of the Côte d'Or, and the 219 different vineyards of the Napa Valley? I hope you have, so you can begin to memorize the more than 1,400 wine villages and over 2,600 vineyards of Germany. No problem, right? What's 4,000 simple little names?

Actually, if you were to have studied German wines before 1971, you would have had 30,000 different names to remember. There used to be very small parcels of land owned by many different people; that's why so many names were involved.

In an effort to make German wines less confusing, the government stepped in and passed a law in 1971. The new ruling stated that a vineyard must encompass at least 12.5 acres of land. This law cut the list of names considerably, although many of the vineyards today still are divided among several owners.

Germany produces only 2 or 3 percent of the world's wines. (Beer, remember, is the national beverage.) And what wines it *does* produce depends largely on the weather. Why is this? Well, look at where the wines are geographically. Germany is the northernmost country in which vines can grow. And 80 percent of the vineyards are located on hilly slopes. They can forget about mechanical harvesting.

With the reunification of Germany in 1989, there are now thirteen different regions that produce wine.

There has been a 10% increase in the vineyards planted over the last ten years.

In Germany, 100,000 grape-growers cultivate nearly 240,000 acres of vines.

The average holding per grower is 2.4 acres.

One mechanical harvester can do the work of 60 people.

The chart below should help give you a better idea of the hilly conditions vintners must contend with in order to grow grapes and produce German wines.

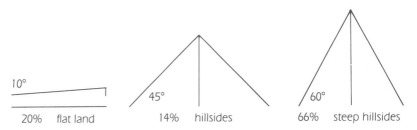

10°	45°	60°
20% flat land	14% hillsides	66% steep hillsides

What are some of the problems of German wines in the American market?

For many people, German wines are not dry enough, especially to drink with most meals. Importers of German wines are trying to respond to this problem. They've been making drier wines: *trocken* (dry) and *halbtrocken* (semi-dry), *and* they're being imported. For the 1990 vintage, 45% of German wine production was *trocken* and *halbtrocken*.

Have you ever noticed that German wines have unpronounceable names? Peter Sichel, the largest exporter of German wines in the world, was one of the first exporters to make German names simpler for Americans. He realized we just weren't buying those wines with the hard-to-pronounce names, so he introduced Blue Nun. It is actually a Liebfraumilch wine, which translated means "milk of the blessed Mother." It's been popular in the United States for many years for many reasons: It's a nice, drinkable wine; it's consistent from year to year; it's very reasonably priced; and it's a lot easier to ask for than Liebfraumilch!

Would You Believe?

Fifty years ago, most German wines were dry and very high in acidity. Even in the finest restaurants, you'd be offered a spoonful of sugar with a German wine to balance the acidity.

What's the style of German wines?

A balance of sweetness with acidity and low alcohol. Remember the equation:

$$\text{Sugar} + \text{Yeast} = \text{Alcohol} + CO_2$$

Where does the sugar come from? The sun! If you have a good year, and your vines are on a southerly slope, you'll get a lot of sun, and therefore the right sugar content to produce a good wine. In many years, however, the winemakers aren't so fortunate and they don't have enough sun to ripen the grapes. The result: higher acidity and lower alcohol. To compensate for this, the winemakers may add sugar to the must before fermentation to increase the amount of alcohol. As mentioned before, this process is called *chaptalization*. (*Note:* Chaptalization is not permitted for higher-quality German wines.)

With German wines, 85 is the important number to remember.

—85% of the wines Germany produces are white.

—If a wine label gives the grape variety – Riesling, for example – 85% of the wine must be made from the Riesling grape.

—If a German wine shows a vintage on the label, 85% of the grapes used must be from that year.

France produces 10 times as much wine as Germany.

As German winemakers say, "100 days of sun will make a good wine, but 120 days of sun will make a great wine."

German wines tend to be 8–10% alcohol, compared to an average 11–13% for French wine.

A Note on Süss-Reserve

A common misconception about German wine is that fermentation stops and the remaining residual sugar gives the wine its sweetness naturally. On the contrary, the wines are fermented dry, and most German winemakers hold back a certain percentage of unfermented grape juice (called Süss-Reserve). This contains all the natural sugar and it's added back to the wine after fermentation. This adds sweetness to the wine and lowers the alcohol content.

What are the main winemaking regions of Germany?

There are 13 winemaking regions. Do you have to commit them all to memory like the hundreds of other names I've mentioned in the book so far? Absolutely not. Why should you worry about all 13 when you only need to be familiar with four? Look at the 13 regions on the map for your own curiosity, but here are the four most important:

Mosel-Saar-Ruwer
Rheingau
Rheinhessen
Pfalz (until 1992, known as Rheinpfalz)

If you were to look at a map of the world, put your finger on Germany, and then follow the 50° north latitude westward across into North America, you'd be pointing to the island of Newfoundland, Canada.

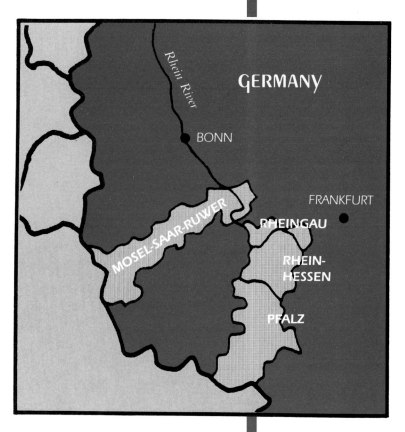

One of the reasons I emphasize these regions above the others is that in the United States you rarely see wine from the other German wine-growing regions. The other reason to look closely at these regions is because they produce the best German wines.

Germany produces red wines, too, but only 15%. Why? Red grapes simply don't grow well in Germany's northerly climate.

What's the difference between Rhein and Mosel wines?

Rhein wines generally have more body than do Mosels. In addition, Mosel wines often have a "spritz"—a natural effervescence. Mosels are also higher in acidity and lower in alcohol than are Rhein wines.

What are the most important grape varieties?

Riesling—This is by far the best grape variety produced in Germany. If you don't see the name "Riesling" on the label, then there's probably very little, if any, Riesling grape in the wine. And remember, if the label gives the grape variety, then there must be at least 85 percent of that grape in the wine, according to German law. Of the grapes planted in Germany, 21 percent are Riesling.

Silvaner—This is another grape variety that accounts for 7 percent of Germany's wines.

Müller-Thurgau—A cross between Riesling and Silvaner, this is the most widely planted grape in Germany.

There are many other grape varieties planted in Germany, and you may be familiar with some of them, such as Gewürztraminer, which is used to make the "spicy" Traminer wine, but for our purposes, we'll concentrate mostly on Riesling.

What are the quality levels of German wine?

As a result of the German law of 1971, there are two main categories of quality. A wine is either *Tafelwein,* which means "table wine," or *Qualitätswein,* "quality wine."

Tafelwein—The lowest designation given to a wine grown in Germany, it never carries the vineyard name. It is rarely seen in the United States.

Qualitätswein—literally, "quality wine."

1. *Qualitätswein bestimmter Anbaugebiete:* I'm giving you this one because you often see the abbreviation QbA on a label. QbA indicates a quality wine that comes from one of the 13 specified regions.

2. *Qualitätswein mit Prädikat:* This is quality wine with distinction—the good stuff. These wines may *not* be chaptalized: The winemaker is not permitted to add sugar. In ascending order of quality, price, and ripeness at harvest, here are the QmP levels:

Kabinett—Light, semi-dry wines made from normally ripened grapes. Cost: $9–$12.

Spätlese—Breaking up the word, *spät* means "late" and *lese* means "picking." Put them together and you have "late picking." That's exactly what the wine is made of—grapes that were picked after the normal harvest. The extra days of sun give the wine more ripeness and a more intense flavor. Cost: $11–$14.

Landwein—A new and higher category of table wine, which must have a higher concentration of grape sugar and can come only from certain areas. It will be either dry or semi-dry (trocken or halbtrocken).

Given good weather, the longer the grapes remain on the vine, the sweeter they become—but the winemaker takes a risk when he does this because all could be lost in the event of bad weather.

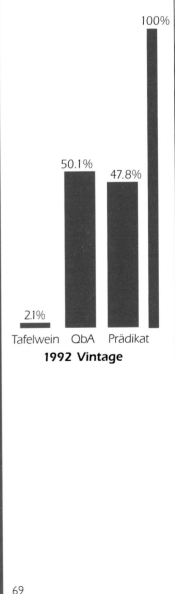

1992 Vintage

MOSEL-SAAR-RUWER
RIESLING
Product of Germany

Scharzhofberger Spätlese

Grand Prix Paris 1900
Grand Prize St. Louis 1904

Erzeugerabfüllung Egon Müller zu Scharzhof

Abgefüllt im
Keller zu Scharzhof.
D 5516 Wiltingen

Qualitätswein mit Prädikat A:c. 9.0% by Vol.   A. P. Nr. 3 567 142-17-91   750 ml

Auslese—Translated as "out picked," this means that the grapes are selectively picked out from particularly ripe bunches. You probably do the same thing in your own garden if you grow tomatoes: You pick out the especially ripe ones, leaving the others on the vine. Cost: $15–$25.

Beerenauslese—Breaking the word down, you get *beeren,* or "berries," *aus,* or "out," and *lese,* or "picking." Quite simply (and don't let the bigger names fool you), these are berries (grapes) that are picked out individually. These luscious grapes are used to create the rich dessert wines for which Germany is known. Beerenauslese is usually made only two or three times every ten years. It's not unheard of for a good Beerenauslese to cost up to $250.

Trockenbeerenauslese—A step above the Beerenauslese, but these grapes are dried (*trocken*), so they're more like raisins. Those "raisinated" grapes produce the richest, sweetest, honey-like wine—and the most expensive, too.

Eiswein—A very rare, sweet, concentrated wine made from frozen grapes left on the vine. They're pressed while still frozen. According to Germany's 1971 rules for winemaking, this wine must now be made from grapes that are at least ripe enough to make a Beerenauslese.

What's the difference between a $50 Beerenauslese and a $150 Beerenauslese (besides $100)?

The major difference is the grapes. The $50 bottle is probably made from Müller-Thurgau grapes or Silvaner, while the $150 bottle is from Riesling. In addition, the region the wine comes from will, in part, determine its quality. Traditionally, the best Beerenauslese and Trockenbeerenauslese come from the Rhein Valley. The most expensive come from the Rheingau.

Today, most German wines, including Beerenauslese and Trockenbeerenauslese, are bottled in spring and early summer. They no longer receive additional cask or tank maturation, because it has been discovered that this extra barrel maturation destroys the fruit.

What Is Botrytis Cinerea?

Botrytis cinerea, known as *Edelfäule* in German, is a mould that (under special conditions) attacks grapes, as was described in the section on Sauternes. I say "special" because this "noble rot" is instrumental in the production of better wines, namely Beerenauslese and Trockenbeerenauslese.

Noble rot occurs late in the growing season when the nights are cool and heavy with dew, the mornings have fog, and the days are warm. When noble rot attacks the grapes, they begin to shrivel and the water evaporates, leaving concentrated sugar. (Remember, 90 percent of wine is water.) Grapes affected by this mould may not look very appealing, but don't let looks deceive you: The proof is in the wine.

When I'm ordering a German wine in a restaurant, or shopping at my local retailer, what should I look for?

The first thing I would make sure of is that it comes from either the Mosel-Saar-Ruwer or the Rheingau region, which, in my opinion, are the most important quality wine-producing regions in all of Germany. These wines are the German equivalent to wines from the Napa Valley, Bordeaux, Burgundy, and so forth.

Some important villages to look for:

Rheingau

Eltville

Erbach

Rüdesheim

Rauenthal

Hochheim

Johannisberg

Mosel-Saar-Ruwer

Piesport

Bernkastel

Graach

Wehlen

Ockfen

Serrig

Zeltingen

Famous vineyards of the Rheingau are:
Schloss Johannisberg
Schloss Vollrads
Steinberg

Famous vineyards of the Mosel-Saar-Ruwer are:
Bernkasteler Doktor
Goldtröpfchen (Piesport)
Scharzhofberg
Sonnenuhr (Wehlen)

Next, look to see if the wine is a Riesling. Anyone who studies and enjoys German wines finds that Riesling shows the best-tasting characteristics. Riesling on the label is a mark of quality.

Finally, be aware of the vintage. It's important, especially with German wines, to know if the wine was made in a good year.

Can you take the mystery out of reading German wine labels?

German wine labels give you plenty of information. For example, see the label below.

Impress your friends with this trivia:

A.P. Nr. 2 606 319 002 93

 2 = the government referral office or testing station
606 = location code of bottler
319 = bottler ID number
002 = bottle lot
 93 = the year the wine was tasted by the board

1. Mosel-Saar-Ruwer—This is the region of the wine's origin. Note that this region is one of the big four we discussed earlier in the chapter.

2. 1992—The year the grapes were harvested.

3. Zeltingen is the town and Sonnenuhr is the vineyard from which the grapes originate. The Germans add the suffix "er" to make Zeltinger, just as a person from New York is called a New Yorker.

4. Spätlese is the style of wine made from late-harvested grapes.

5. Riesling is the grape variety. Therefore, this wine is at least 85 percent Riesling.

6. Qualitätswein mit Prädikat is the quality level of the wine.

7. A.P. Nr. 2 606 319 002 93 is the official testing number—proof that the wine was tasted by a panel of tasters and passed the strict quality standards required by the government.

8. Erzeugerabfüllung means estate-bottled.

9. Selbach-Oster is the wine's producer.

What are the trends in the white wines of Germany over the last ten years?

As Americans' drinking tastes have shifted from generic wines to varietal wines, and so also towards drier wines, we've seen a decrease in the availability of German wines in the American market. German wines have also been hampered in the American market by the increase in their prices. Still, I feel the lighter-style German Kabinetts and even Spätleses are wines that can be easily served as an apéritif, or with very light food and also grilled food.

It's extremely rare in a northerly climate such as Germany's to have three great vintages in a row, but such was the case in 1988, 1989, and 1990.

Best Bets for Recent Vintages in Germany

1985   1988   1989   1990   1992   1993

WINE AND Food

Rainer Lingenfelder (Weingut Lingenfelder Estate, Pfalz) – With Riesling Spätlese Halbtrocken: "We have a tradition of cooking freshwater fish which come from a number of small creeks in the Palatinate forest, so my personal choice would be trout, either herbed with thyme, basil, parsley, and onion, and cooked in wine, or smoked with a bit of horseradish. We find it to be a very versatile wine, which is a very good match with a whole range of white meat. Pork is traditional in the Palatinate region, as are chicken and goose dishes."

Johannes Selbach (Selbach-Oster, Mosel) – "What kinds of food do we have with Riesling Spätlese? Anything we like! This may sound funny but there's a wide variety of foods which go very well with a – and this is the key – fruity, only moderately sweet, well-balanced Riesling Spätlese. Start with mild curries and sesame- or ginger-flavored not-too-spicy dishes.

For *haute cuisine,* fresh duck or goose liver lightly sauteed in its own juice, or veal sweetbreads in a rich sauce. Also salads with fresh greens, fresh fruit, and fresh seafood marinated in lime or lemon juice or balsamic vinegar.

With an old ripe Spätlese: roast venison, dishes with cream sauces, and any white meat dish stuffed with or accompanied by fruit. It is also delicious with fresh fruit itself or as an aperitif.

With Riesling Spätlese Halbtrocken: This is a food-friendly wine, but the first thing that comes to mind is fresh seafood and fresh fish. Also wonderful with salads with a mild vinaigrette, and with a course that's often difficult to match: cream soups. If we don't know exactly what to drink with a particular food, Spätlese Halbtrocken is usually the safe bet.

73

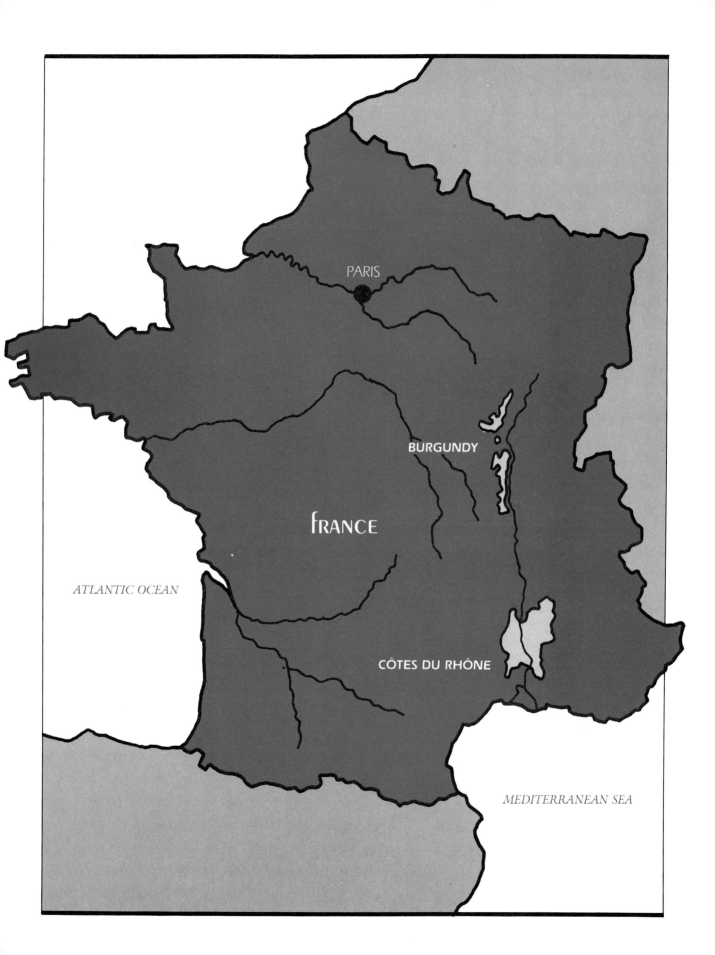

THE Red WINES of bURGUNDY AND THE RHÔNE VALLEY

Now we're getting into a whole new experience in wines—the reds. Generally, my students and I become more intense and concentrate more when we taste red wines.

What's so different (beyond the obvious color)?

We're beginning to see more components in the wines—more complexities. In the white wines, we were looking mainly for the acid/fruit balance, but now, in addition, we're looking for other characteristics, such as tannin.

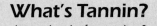

What's Tannin?

Tannin is what gives wine its longevity. It comes from the skins, the pits, and the stems of the grapes. Another source of tannin is wood, especially the French oak barrels in which some wines are aged.

A word used to describe the taste sensation of tannin is "astringent." Let an aspirin dissolve in your mouth and you'll understand what I mean.

Tannin is also found in strong tea. And what can you add to the tea to make it less astringent? Milk—it softens the tannin. And so it is with a highly tannic wine. If you take another milk by-product, such as cheese, and have it with wine, it softens the tannin and makes the wine more appealing.

THE RED WINES of BURGUNDY

Why is Burgundy so difficult to understand?

Before we go any further, I must tell you that there are no short-cuts. Burgundy is one of the most difficult subjects in the study of wines. People get uptight about Burgundy. They say, "There's so much to know," and "It looks so hard." Yes, there are many vineyards and villages, and they're all important. But actually, there are only 15 to 25 names you need to familiarize yourself with, if you'd like to know and speak about Burgundy wines intelligently. Not to worry. I'm going to help you decode all the mysteries of Burgundy: names, regions, and labels.

What are the main red-wine-producing areas of Burgundy?

Côte d'Or { Côte de Nuits   Beaujolais
           { Côte de Beaune   Côte Châlonnaise

What major grape varieties are used in red Burgundy wines?

The two major grape varieties are Pinot Noir and Gamay. Under Appellation Contrôlée laws, all red Burgundies, excluding Beaujolais, must be made from the Pinot Noir grape. Beaujolais is produced from the Gamay grape variety.

Let's take a closer look at the red-wine-producing regions of Burgundy.

beaujolais

Made from 100 percent Gamay grapes, this wine's style is typically light and fruity. It's meant to be consumed young. Beaujolais is the largest-selling Burgundy in the United States by far, probably because it's so easy to drink. It can be chilled, and it's very affordable. Most bottles cost between $6 and $10, although the price varies with the quality and the grade.

What are the quality levels of Beaujolais?

Beaujolais—the basic Beaujolais. The only difference between this wine and Beaujolais Supérieur is that Supérieur has more alcohol, but the quality is the same. The basic Beaujolais accounts for the majority of all Beaujolais produced (Cost: $).

Beaujolais-Villages—comes from certain villages in Beaujolais. There are 35 villages that consistently produce better wines. Most Beaujolais-

Villages is a blend of wines from these villages, and usually no particular village name is included on the label (Cost: $$).

"Cru"—a total of ten in Beaujolais. A "cru" is actually the name of a village that produces the highest quality of Beaujolais (Cost: $$$$).

Here are the ten "crus" (villages):

Brouilly
Morgon
Moulin-à-Vent } These four are the most popular of the "crus" and account for 60 percent of Beaujolais "cru" production.
Fleurie
Côte de Brouilly
Chiroubles
Chénas
Juliénas
Saint-Amour
Régnié

Wines from the ten "crus" of Beaujolais usually do not bear the name "Beaujolais" on the label—just the name of the village. This is because the producers of "cru" Beaujolais don't want to have their wines confused with basic Beaujolais.

What's Beaujolais Nouveau?

Beaujolais Nouveau is a fruity, light-style wine that's best drunk young. Isn't that true of *all* Beaujolais wines? Yes, but Nouveau is different. This "new" Beaujolais is picked, fermented, bottled, and available at your local retailer in a matter of weeks. (I don't know what you call that in your business, but I call it good cash flow in mine. It gives the winemaker virtually an instant return.)

There's another purpose behind Beaujolais Nouveau: It gives the public a sample of the quality and style that the winemaker produces in his regular Beaujolais.

Beaujolais Nouveau is meant to be consumed within six months of bottling. So if you're holding a 1985 Beaujolais Nouveau, now is the time to give it to your "friends."

One-third of the Beaujolais crop is used to make Beaujolais Nouveau, but Beaujolais Nouveau represents half of all exports of that crop.

Beaujolais Nouveau Madness

The exact date of release is the third Thursday in November, and Beaujolais Nouveau is introduced to the consumer amidst great hoopla. The restaurants and retailers all vie to be the first to offer the new Beaujolais to their customers. Some of these wine buyers go so far as to fly the wine into the United States on the Concorde.

How long should I keep a Beaujolais?

It depends on the level of quality and the vintage. Beaujolais is meant to last between one and two years, except for the "cru" Beaujolais. "Crus" can last longer because they are more complex. I've tasted Beaujolais "crus" that were more than 10 years old and still in excellent condition. This is the exception, though, not the rule.

Which shippers/producers should I look for when buying Beaujolais?

Bouchard   Drouhin   Duboeuf   Jadot   Mommessin

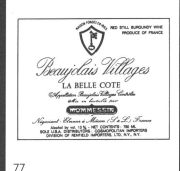

To Chill or Not to Chill?

As a young student studying wines in Burgundy, I visited the Beaujolais region, excited and naive. In one of the towns, I stopped at a bistro and ordered a glass of Beaujolais. (A good choice on my part, don't you think?) The waiter brought the glass of Beaujolais and it was *chilled*, and I thought to myself that these people had not read the proper books! Every wine book I'd ever read always said you serve red wines at room temperature and white wines chilled.

Obviously, I learned from my experience that when it comes to Beaujolais Nouveau, Beaujolais, and Beaujolais-Villages, it's a good idea to give them a slight chill to bring out the fruit and liveliness (acidity) of the wines, making them probably the best red wines to have during the summer.

However, to my taste, the Beaujolais "crus" have more fruit and more tannin and should not be served chilled.

Best Bets for Recent Vintages of Beaujolais
1992   1993   1994

wine and food

Beaujolais goes well with almost anything—especially light, simple meals and cheeses—nothing overpowering. Generally, try to match your Beaujolais with light food, such as veal, fish, or fowl. Here's what some of the experts say:

Jean-François Bouchard—"A perfect picnic wine; good for the first course, charcuterie, cold meats, and salads."

André Gagey (Louis Jadot)—"Beaujolais with simple meals, light cheeses, grilled meat—everything except sweets."

Georges Duboeuf—"A lot of dishes can be eaten with Beaujolais–what you choose depends on the appellation and vintage. With charcuteries and pâtés you can serve a young Beaujolais or Beaujolais Villages. With grilled meat, more generous and fleshy wines, such as Juliénas and Morgon crus, can be served. With meats cooked in a sauce (for example, coq au vin), I would suggest a Moulin à Vent cru from a good vintage."

Didier Mommessin—"Serve with an extremely strong cheese, such as Roquefort, especially when the wine is young and strong enough for it. Also with white meat and veal."

"Beaujolais is one of the very few red wines that can be drunk as a white. Beaujolais is my daily drink. And sometimes I blend one-half water to the wine. It is the most refreshing drink in the world."—Didier Mommessin

CÔTE CHÂLONNAISE

You should know three villages from this area:
Mercurey   Givry   Rully

Mercurey is the most important, producing wines of high quality. Because they are not well known in the United States, Mercurey wines are often a very good buy.

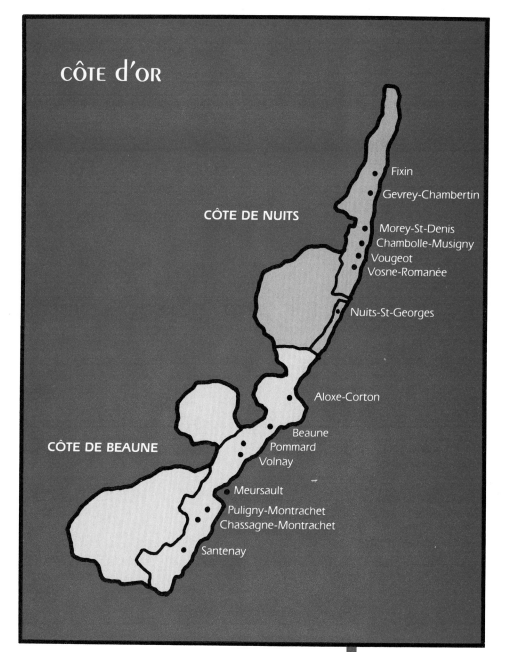

CÔTE d'OR

Fixin
Gevrey-Chambertin
Morey-St-Denis
Chambolle-Musigny
Vougeot
Vosne-Romanée
Nuits-St-Georges
CÔTE DE NUITS
Aloxe-Corton
Beaune
Pommard
Volnay
CÔTE DE BEAUNE
Meursault
Puligny-Montrachet
Chassagne-Montrachet
Santenay

CÔTE d'OR

Now we're getting to the heart of Burgundy. The Côte d'Or (pronounced "coat door") means "golden slope." One reason this name is appropriate is because of the color of the foliage on the hillside in autumn. Another reason this region is golden is because of the income it brings the winemakers—the wines aren't exactly $2.99! The Côte d'Or is divided into two regions:

Côte de Beaune—red and white wines

Côte de Nuits—the highest quality red Burgundy wines come from this region

The Côte d'Or is only 30 miles long and a half-mile wide.

79

What's the best way to understand the wines of the Côte d'Or?

First, you need to know that these wines are distinguished by quality levels—Generic, Village, Premier Cru and Grand Cru. Let's look at the quality levels with the "double pyramid" shown below. As you can see, not much Grand Cru wine is produced, but that small amount is top quality. Generic, on the other hand, is available in abundance. Although much is produced, very few generic wines can be classified as "outstanding."

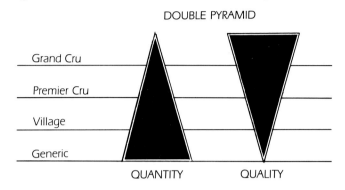

DOUBLE PYRAMID

Grand Cru
Premier Cru
Village
Generic

QUANTITY   QUALITY

Another way to understand the wines of the Côte d'Or is to become familiar with the most important villages, grand cru vineyards, and some of the premier cru vineyards.

CÔTE DE BEAUNE

Villages	My Favorite Premier Cru Vinyards	Grand Cru Vineyards
Aloxe-Corton	Maréchaude	Corton
	Fournières	Corton Clos du Roi
	Chaillots	Corton Bressandes
		Corton Renardes
Beaune	Grèves	None
	Fèves	
	Marconnets	
	Bressandes	
	Clos des Mouches	
Pommard	Epenots	None
	Rugiens	
Volnay	Caillerets	None
	Santenots	
	Clos des Chênes	

A good trivia question for your friends: How many red grands crus are there in the Côte de Beaune? Answer: Only one—Corton, from the village of Aloxe-Corton.

Generic wines are labelled simply "Burgundy" or "Bourgogne."

There are hundreds of premier cru vineyards.

ALOXE CORTON LATOUR
APPELLATION ALOXE-CORTON CONTROLÉE
MIS EN BOUTEILLE PAR
LOUIS LATOUR, NÉGOCIANT A BEAUNE (CÔTE D'OR)

By far the largest grand cru, in terms of production, is Corton, representing about 25 percent of all Grand cru red wines.

CÔTE DE NUITS

Finally, we reach the Côte de Nuits. If you're going to spend any time studying your geography, do it now. Most of the big, full-bodied reds come from this area. The most important names (also the most expensive) to remember when you go to your local retailer or dine out are:

Wines from Mazoyères-Chambertin are legally entitled to be labelled Charmes-Chambertin.

Village	My Favorite Premier Cru Vineyards	Grand Cru Vineyards
Gevrey-Chambertin	Clos St-Jacques	Chambertin
	Les Cazetiers	Chambertin Clos de Bèze
	Aux Combottes	Latricières-Chambertin
		Mazis-Chambertin
		Mazoyères-Chambertin
		Ruchottes-Chambertin
		Chapelle-Chambertin
		Charmes-Chambertin
		Griotte-Chambertin

Joseph Drouhin

CHAMBERTIN - CLOS DE BÈZE

APPELLATION CONTROLÉE

MIS EN BOUTEILLE PAR

JOSEPH DROUHIN
Maison fondée en 1880

NÉGOCIANT A BEAUNE, COTE-D'OR

AUX CELLIERS DES ROIS DE FRANCE ET DES DUCS DE BOURGOGNE

Chambertin Clos de Bèze was the favorite wine of Napoléon, who is reported to have said: "Nothing makes the future look so rosy as to contemplate it through a glass of Chambertin." Obviously, he ran out of Chambertin at Waterloo!

Morey-St-Denis	Ruchots	Clos des Lambrays
	Les Genevrières	Clos de Tart
	Clos des Ormes	Clos St-Denis
		Clos de la Roche
		Bonnes Mares (part)
Chambolle-Musigny	Les Amoureuses	Musigny
	Charmes	Bonnes Mares (part)
Vougeot		Clos de Vougeot
Flagey-Échézeaux		Échézeaux
		Grands-Échézeaux
Vosne-Romanée	Beaux-Monts	Grande-Rue
	Malconsorts	Romanée-Conti
		La Romanée
		La Tâche
		Richebourg
		Romanée-St-Vivant
Nuits-St-Georges	Les St-Georges	None
	Vaucrains	
	Porets	

The Newest Grand Cru—In July 1992, La Grande-Rue, a vineyard tucked between the grands crus La Tâche and Romanée-Conti in Vosne-Romanée, was itself elevated to the grand cru level, bringing the number of grands crus in the Côte d'Or to 32.

The smallest grand cru is La Romanée, representing less than one quarter of one percent of all red grand cru wines.

MIS EN BOUTEILLE AU DOMAINE

PRODUCE OF FRANCE

APPELLATION CONTROLÉE

NUITS ST GEORGES

Les St-Georges

750 ml

Domaine Henri Gouges à Nuits St Georges
(Côte-d'Or)   FRANCE   Bourgogne

If you look at a map, you'll notice that there are many more names. I'm only listing the main ones you need to know—to make life easier.

The Importance of Soil to Burgundy Wines

If you talk to any producers of Burgundy wines, they'll tell you the most important element in making their quality wines is the soil in which the grapes are grown. This, together with the slope of the land (and the sunshine), determines whether the wine is a Village wine, a Premier Cru, or a Grand Cru.

During one of my trips to Burgundy, it rained for five straight days. On the sixth day I saw that the workers were at the bottom of the slopes with their pails and shovels, collecting the soil that had run down the hillside and returning the soil to the vineyard.

Why are we bothering with all this geography? Must we learn the names of all the villages and vineyards?

I thought you'd never ask. First of all, the geography is important because it helps make you a smart buyer. If you're familiar with the most important villages and vineyards, you're more likely to make an educated purchase.

You really don't have to memorize *all* the villages and vineyards. I'll let you in on a little secret of how to choose a Burgundy wine and tell at a glance if it's a Village wine, a Premier Cru, or a Grand Cru—usually the label will tip you off in the manner illustrated here:

Village (only)
= Village wine

Village + Vineyard
= Premier Cru

Vineyard (only)
= Grand Cru

Has this ever happened to you? In a restaurant, you order a village wine—Chambolle Musigny, for example—and the waiter brings you a Grand Cru Musigny. What would you do?

82

This is the method I use to teach Burgundy wine. Ask yourself the following:

Where is the wine from?

France.

What type of wine is it?

Burgundy.

Which region is it from?

Côte d'Or.

Which area?

Côte de Nuits.

Which village is the wine from?

Vosne-Romanée.

Does the label give more details?

Yes, it tells you that the wine is from a vineyard called La Tâche, which is designated as a grand cru vineyard.

SOCIÉTÉ CIVILE DU DOMAINE DE LA ROMANÉE-CONTI
PROPRIÉTAIRE A VOSNE-ROMANÉE (COTE-D'OR) FRANCE

LA TÂCHE

APPELLATION LA TÂCHE CONTROLÉE

24.071 Bouteilles Récoltées

BOUTEILLE N°

ANNÉE

LES ASSOCIÉS-GÉRANTS

Charles Roch
A. de Villaine

Mise en bouteille au domaine

France ——————
Burgundy ————
Côte d'Or ————
Côte de Nuits ————
Vosne-Romanée ————
La Tâche ————

$$

After we finish the class about Burgundy at Windows on the World and everyone has tasted our selections of the evening, my students often ask:

Has the style of Burgundy wines changed in the last 25 years?

There is a good deal of debate about this in the wine industry. I would have to answer that, yes, it has indeed changed. Winemakers used to make Burgundies to last longer. In fact, you couldn't drink a Burgundy for several years, if you wanted to get the fullest flavor. It simply wasn't ready. Today the winemakers of Burgundy are complying with consumer demand for Burgundy they can drink earlier. In America, it seems no one has the patience to wait. A compromise had to be made, however, and that is in the body. Many wines are lighter in style and they can be consumed just a few years after the vintage.

In Burgundy in the 1960s, wines were fermented and vatted for up to three weeks. Today's Burgundy wines are usually fermented for six to twelve days.

83

Why are the well-known great Burgundies so expensive?

The answer is simple—supply and demand. The Burgundy growers and shippers of the Côte d'Or have a problem all business people would envy—not enough supply to meet the demand. It has been this way for years and it will continue, because Burgundy is a small region that produces a limited amount of wine. The Bordeaux wine region produces three times as much wine as Burgundy does.

Take a look at the following wine harvest chart. It gives you a better idea of the limited supply of Burgundy wine. The region's wine production is broken down into cases. For instance, if you look under "Grands Crus of the Côte de Nuits" and find La Tâche, you'll see that less than 1,500 cases of wine were produced. That's not very much for world consumption—of course, it's an expensive wine.

If you don't want to be disappointed by the Burgundy wine you select, make sure you know your vintages. Also, due to the delicacy of the Pinot Noir grape, red Burgundies require proper storage, so make sure you buy from a merchant who handles Burgundy wines with care.

"To Decant, or not to Decant?" It has been my experience that in Burgundy, wine is rarely decanted, whereas in Bordeaux, it is almost always decanted. (More about decanting on page 175.)

Burgundy Wine Harvest

(average number of cases over a five-year period)

	RED	WHITE
REGIONAL APPELLATIONS	1,851,120	625,264
Chablis		
Petit Chablis		42,757
Chablis		419,491
Premier Cru		243,878
Grand Cru		49,062
		755,188
COTE D'OR		
Côte de Nuits		
Chambolle-Musigny	43,700	
Gevrey-Chambertin	145,787	
Morey-St-Denis	22,899	233
Nuits-St-Georges	82,695	166
Vougeot	4,040	477
Vosne-Romanée	51,426	
Other	69,086	
	419,633	876
Côte de Beaune		
Aloxe-Corton	45,865	178
Auxey-Duress	35,698	11,699
Beaune	121,545	5,528
Chassagne-Montrachet	79,132	58,375
Fixin	13,364	
Meursault	9,368	167,654
Pommard	104,772	

Puligny–Montrachet	3,374	99,212
Santenay	116,317	1,754
Volnay	79,609	
Other	365,233	30,414
	974,277	376,757
Côte Châlonnaise	285,436	72,103
Mâconnais		
Pouilly-Fuissé		358,908
Other	597,003	1,180,763
	597,003	1,539,671
Beaujolais	8,255,070	56,399
Beaujolais Villages and Crus	3,192,148	

Selected Grands Crus of the Côte de Nuits

Bonne Mares	3,740	
Chambertin	5,483	
Chambertin Clos de Bèze	4,717	
Chapelle-Chambertin	2,086	
Charmes-Chambertin	10,254	
Clos de la Roche	4,872	
Clos St-Denis	1,731	
Clos de Tart	1,875	
Clos de Vougeot	13,908	
Échézaux	10,922	
Grands-Échézaux	2,609	
Griotte-Chambertin	666	
La Tâche	1,487	
Latricières-Chambertin	2,541	
Mazis-Chambertin	2,297	
Musigny	2,397	66
Richebourg	2,353	
La Romanée	210	
Romanée-Conti	499	
Romanée-St-Vivant	2,231	
Ruchottes-Chambertin	777	—
	77,655	66

Selected Grands Crus of the Côte de Beaune

Bâtard-Montrachet		5,128
Bienvenue-Bâtard-Montrachet		1,431
Chevalier-Montrachet		2,020
Corton	28,216	477
Corton-Charlemagne		13,197
Criots-Bâtard-Montrachet		521
Montrachet		2,508
	28,216	25,282
	15,680,558	3,451,606
		15,680,558
		3,451,606

BURGUNDY WINE PRODUCTION **19,132,164 cases**

Who are the most important shippers to look for when buying red Burgundy wine?

Bouchard Père et Fils

Joseph Drouhin

Jaffelin

Louis Jadot

Louis Latour

Moillard

Labouré-Roi

Although 80 percent of Burgundy wine is sold through shippers, some fine estate-bottled wines are available in limited quantities in the United States. Look for the following:

Maison Faiveley (Côte Châlonnaise)

Domaine Daniel Rion
Domaine Henri Gouges } (Nuits-St-Georges)

Domaine Prince de Merode (Aloxe-Corton)

Domaine Dujac
Domaine Georges Roumier } (Morey-St-Denis)

Domaine Louis Trapet
Domaine Pierre Damoy } (Gevrey-Chambertin)

Domaine de La Romanée-Conti
Domaine Henri Lamarche } (Vosne-Romanée)
Domaine Mongeard-Mugneret

Domaine Leroy (Auxey-Duress)

Domaine Comte de Voguë (Chambolle-Musigny)

Domaine Clerget
Domaine Parent } (Pommard)

What are the trends in the red wines of Burgundy over the last ten years?

When I first started studying wines 25 years ago, I had a "love affair" with the red wines of Burgundy. In the early 1970s, I had a "divorce" from Burgundy, and I didn't rekindle my interest until the 1985 vintage came along, followed by the 1988, 1989, and 1990. I've been brought back to the quality, easy drinkability, and elegance of the Pinot Noir grape, along with its great accessibility with food. That's the good news.

The bad news is that the prices are still extremely high for Côte d'Or wines.

Beaujolais is still one of my favorite "drinking" wines. It still maintains its price levels throughout the United States, making it one of the best values in the world for a red wine.

Both Burgundy and Beaujolais represent much better styles of wine to have with the lighter fare or lighter foods that have been promoted over the last ten years. Red Burgundy is the perfect wine to have with fish! In a restaurant, there's no doubt in my mind that I would go more for a Pinot Noir than for a Cabernet Sauvignon. That is, I'll take wines from Cabernet Sauvignon and put them in my own wine cellar, but when going to a restaurant I will definitely order a wine in the lighter—and more accessible—style of a Pinot Noir/Burgundy.

Wine and Food

To get the most flavor from both the wine and the food, some of Burgundy's famous winemakers offer these suggestions:

Jean-François Bouchard—"Lamb cooked in its own sauce—not too spicy . . . or veal with mushroom sauce."

Robert Drouhin—"For light red Burgundies, white meat—not too many spices; partridge, pheasant, and rabbit. For heavier-style wines, lamb and steak are good choices." Personally, Mr. Drouhin does not enjoy red Burgundies with cheese—especially goat cheese.

André Gagey(Louis Jadot)—"For lighter-style wines such as Volnay—roast chicken, roast duck, and veal. For big wines such as Corton, Gevrey-Chambertin, Chambolle-Musigny—venison or steak cooked with red wine. For older Burgundian wines—goat cheese, or Gruyère, or Brie."

Louis Latour—"Red wines need strong foods, such as venison, duck, or chicken in a red wine sauce."

For further reading on Burgundy wines, I recommend *Burgundy*, by Anthony Hanson, *Burgundy*, by Robert M. Parker, Jr., *Making Sense of Burgundy*, by Matt Kramer, and *The Great Domaines of Burgundy*, by Remington Norman.

THE RED WINES OF THE RHÔNE VALLEY

Many times at Windows on the World customers asked me to recommend a big robust red Burgundy wine to complement their Chateaubriand or filet mignon. To their surprise, I didn't recommend a Burgundy at all. Their best bet was a Rhône wine.

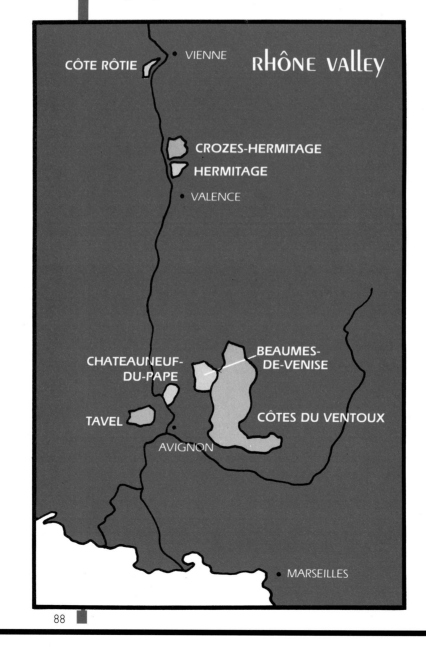

What's a Rhône wine?

A Rhône wine is typically a bigger, fuller wine than one from Burgundy, and it has a higher alcoholic content. The reason for this is quite simple. It all goes back to location—geography.

Where's the Rhône Valley?

The Rhône Valley is in southeastern France, south of the Burgundy region. Here the climate is hot and the conditions are sunny. The extra sun gives the wines that added boost of alcohol, because, as you know, the sun gives the grapes the sugar that turns into alcohol. The soil is full of rocks that retain the intense summer heat during both day and night.

I just told you that Rhône wines are known to have more alcohol than other French wines. That's a fact. It's also a fact that the winemakers of the Rhône Valley are required by law to make sure their wines have a specified amount of alcohol. For example, the minimum alcoholic content required by the A.O.C. is 10.5 percent for Côtes du Rhône and 12.5 percent for Châteauneuf-du-Pape.

What are the winemaking regions in the Rhône Valley?

The region is divided into two distinct areas: northern and southern Rhône. Red wines that come from the northern region are:

Côte Rôtie

Crozes–Hermitage

Hermitage

Of all the wines made in the Rhône Valley, 95% are red.

A simple Côtes du Rhône is similar to a Beaujolais wine except the Côtes du Rhône has more body and alcohol. A Beaujolais, by A.O.C. standards, must contain a minimum of 9% alcohol—a Côtes du Rhône, 10.5%.

Some of the oldest vineyards in France are in the Rhône Valley. Hermitage, for example, has been in existence for more than 2,000 years.

Hermitage is the best and the longest-lived of the Rhône wines. In a great vintage, Hermitage wines can last for 50 years.

There is a white Châteauneuf-du-Pape and a white Hermitage, but only a few thousand cases are produced each year.

The two most famous white wines of the Rhône Valley are called Condrieu and Château Grillet. Both are made from the grape variety called Viognier.

For those who prefer sweet wines, try Beaumes-de-Venise. It's a fortified wine made from the Muscat grape.

There is no official classification for Rhône Valley wines.

You may be more familiar with the wines from the southern region:

Côtes du Rhône

Châteauneuf-du-Pape

Tavel

Two distinct microclimates separate the north from the south. It is important for you to understand that these areas make distinctly different wines because of:

1. soil
2. location
3. different grape varieties used in making the wines of each area

What are the main red-grape varieties used in the Rhône Valley?

Now we're going to consider some new grapes:

Grenache
Syrah
Cinsault
Mourvèdre

Which wines are made from these grapes?

The Côte Rôtie, Hermitage, and Crozes-Hermitage from the north are made from the Syrah grape. These are the biggest, fullest wines from that region.

Châteauneuf-du-Pape and Tavel acquire their style primarily from the Grenache grape. For Châteauneuf-du-Pape, as many as thirteen separate grape varieties may be included in the blend, but usually the two predominant grapes are Grenache and Syrah.

What's Tavel?

We've already established that it's made primarily from the Grenache grape, although nine grape varieties can be used in the blend. However, it's a rosé—an unusually dry rosé, which distinguishes it from most others. When you come right down to it, Tavel is just like a red wine with all of the components but less color. How do they make a rosé wine with red-wine characteristics but less color? It's all in the vatting process.

What's the difference between "short-vatted" and "long-vatted" wines?

When a wine is "short-vatted," the skins are allowed to ferment with the must (grape juice) for a short period of time—only long enough to impart that rosé color. It's just the opposite when a winemaker is producing other red Rhône wines, such as Châteauneuf-du-Pape or Hermitage. The grape skins are allowed to ferment with the must for a longer time, giving a rich, ruby color to the wine.

What's the difference between a $15 bottle of Châteauneuf-du-Pape and a $30 bottle of Châteauneuf-du-Pape?

A winemaker is permitted to use thirteen different grapes for his Châteauneuf-du-Pape recipe, as I mentioned earlier. It's only logical, then, that the winemaker who used a lot of the best grapes (which is equivalent to cooking with the finest ingredients) will produce the best-tasting—and the most expensive—wine.

For example, a $15 bottle of Châteauneuf-du-Pape may contain only 20 percent of top-quality grapes (Grenache, Mourvèdre, Syrah, and Cinsault) and 80 percent of lesser-quality grapes; a $30 bottle may contain 90 percent of the top-quality grapes and 10 percent of others.

Châteauneuf-du-Pape means "new castle of the Pope," so named for the palace in the Rhône city of Avignon in which Pope Clément V resided in the fourteenth century.

The papal coat of arms from medieval times appears on some Châteauneuf-du-Pape bottles. Only owners of vineyards are permitted to use this coat of arms on the label.

MIS EN BOUTEILLE DU CHATEAU

Château de Beaucastel

CHATEAUNEUF-DU-PAPE

APPELLATION CHATEAUNEUF-DU-PAPE CONTROLÉE

Sté FERMIÈRE DES VIGNOBLES PIERRE PERRIN
AU CHATEAU DE BEAUCASTEL COURTHEZON (Vse) FRANCE   750 ml
ALC. 13.5% BY VOL.

PRODUCE OF FRANCE

IMPORTED BY **Vineyard Brands, Inc.** CHESTER, VT

SHIPPED BY ROBERT HAAS SELECTIONS, FRANCE

Maybe 1989 is the best year to buy Rhône Valley wines since 1978, both north and south.

Rhône Valley vintages can be tricky: A good year in the north may be a bad year in the south, and vice versa.

La Vieille Ferme·
Côtes du Ventoux
Appellation Côtes du Ventoux Contrôlée
Ventoux Red Wine
Mis en bouteille à la Vieille Ferme

La Vieille Ferme · Route de Jonquères, Orange (Vse) France
750 ml   Produce of France   Alc 12.5% by vol
Imported by **Vineyard-Brands,Inc.** Chester, VT
Shipped by Robert Haas Sélections · France

A good value is Côtes du Ventoux. This relatively new appellation was begun in 1973. The wines that come into the American market are generally less expensive because not too many consumers know about them. One of the most widely available wines to look for in this category is La Vieille Ferme. It's inexpensive and a good value.

How do I buy a red Rhône wine?

You should first decide if you prefer a light Côtes du Rhône wine or a bigger, more flavorful one. Then you must consider the vintage and the producer. Two of the oldest and best-known firms are M. Chapoutier and Paul Jaboulet Aîné. The wines of Guigal, Chave, Beaucastel, and Domaine duVieux Télégraphe are harder to find, but worth the search.

When should I drink my Rhône wine?

Tavel—within two years

Côtes du Rhône—within three years

Crozes-Hermitage—within five years

Châteauneuf-du-Pape—after five years, but higher quality Châteauneuf-du-Pape is better at ten years.

Hermitage—seven to eight years, but best at fifteen, in a great year.

What are the trends in the red wines of the Rhône Valley over the last ten years?

The wines from the Rhône Valley are still some of my favorite wines for their depth of concentration, fruit, and longevity. The biggest change in the famous wines such as Châteauneuf-du-Pape and Hermitage is how the wines have increased in price over the last ten years. Côtes du Rhône still remains a good value, but the other wines don't represent the great values that they used to.

The recognition of the quality of the Rhône wines is evidenced by the winemakers of California, who are now planting not just Cabernets and Pinot Noirs, but also the Syrah, Mourvèdre, and the Viognier for the whites. So the California "Rhône Rangers," as they're known, have discovered the greatness of these wines.

WINE AND food

Gérard Jaboulet—"A simple Côtes du Rhône is good to have with poultry, such as chicken, in a light sauce.

"To have Châteauneuf-du-Pape with food," says Mr. Jaboulet, "the wine must be at least three to four years old." He likes a good simple steak with his Châteauneuf-du-Pape, and says the wine overpowers lamb.

"An aged Hermitage should be reserved for that special evening.

"Tavel should be slightly chilled and is a good picnic wine; it goes especially well with cold chicken." Mr. Jaboulet notes: "As the temperature goes up, so do the Tavel sales."

Michel Chapoutier—With a Côtes du Rhône wine, he recommends poultry, light meats, and cheese.

Côte Rôtie goes well with white meats and small game.

Châteauneuf-du-Pape complements the ripest of cheese, the richest venison, and the most lavish civet of wild boar.

A Hermitage is suitable with beef, game, and any full-flavored cheese.

Tavel rosé is excellent with white meat and poultry.

MONIER DE LA SIZERANNE

HERMITAGE

APPELLATION HERMITAGE CONTRÔLÉE

M. CHAPOUTIER S.A.

NÉGOCIANTS-ELEVEURS A TAIN-L'HERMITAGE (DRÔME) FRANCE

CONTAINS SULFITES · RED BORE WINE

IMPORTED BY PATERNO IMPORTS, LTD. CHICAGO, IL

NET CONTENTS 750 ML · ALCOHOL 12.5% BY VOLUME · PRODUCT OF FRANCE

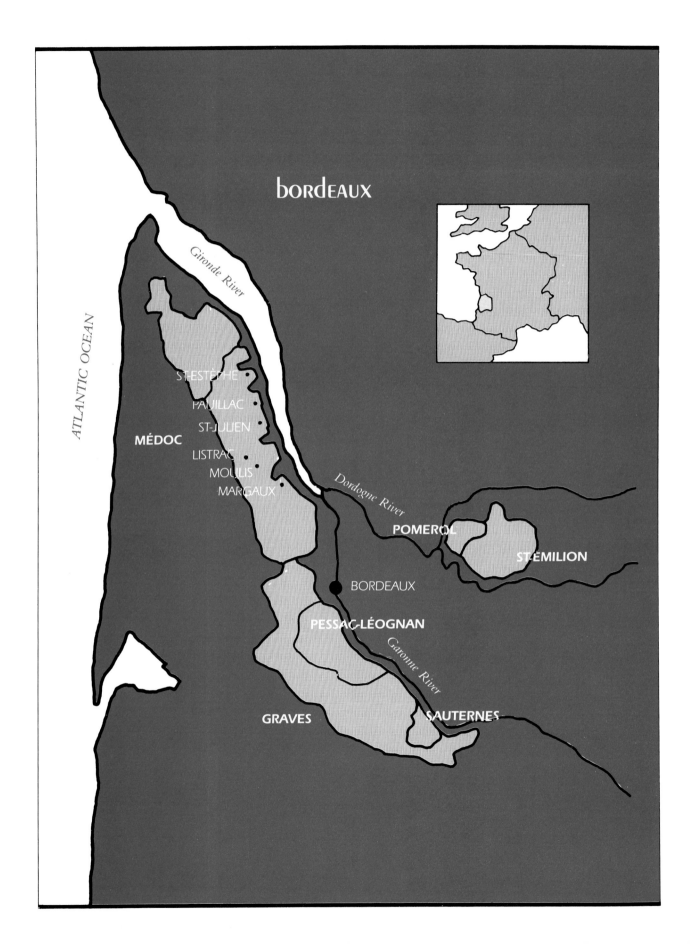

bordeaux

Gironde River

ATLANTIC OCEAN

ST-ESTÈPHE

PAUILLAC

ST-JULIEN

MÉDOC

LISTRAC

MOULIS

MARGAUX

Dordogne River

POMEROL

ST-EMILION

BORDEAUX

PESSAC-LÉOGNAN

Garonne River

GRAVES

SAUTERNES

THE RED WINES of bordeAUX

This province of France is rich with excitement and history, and the best part is that the wines speak for themselves. You'll find this region much easier to learn about than Burgundy. For one thing, the plots of land are bigger, and they're owned by fewer landholders. And, as Samuel Johnson once said, "He who aspires to be a serious wine drinker must drink claret."

Some 53 wine regions in Bordeaux produce high-quality wine that enables them to carry the A.O.C. designation on the label. Of these 53 places, four stand out in my mind for red wine:

> **Médoc**—33,641 acres (produces only red wines)
>
> **Pomerol**—1,803 acres (produces only red wines)
>
> **Graves/Pessac-Léognan**—9,249 acres (produces both red and dry white wines)
>
> **St-Émilion**—12,676 acres (produces only red wines)

In the Médoc, there are seven important *inner* appellations you should be familiar with:

> **Haut Médoc**—9,388 acres
>
> **St-Estèphe**—3,016 acres
>
> **Pauillac**—2,719 acres
>
> **St-Julien**—2,176 acres
>
> **Margaux**—3,162 acres
>
> **Moulis**—1,247 acres
>
> **Listrac**—1,904 acres

The English word "claret" refers to dry red wines from Bordeaux.

Of all the A.O.C. wines of France, 25% come from the Bordeaux region.

Bordeaux is much larger in acreage than Burgundy.

In dollar value, the United States is the second-largest importer of Bordeaux wines: 25% white, 75% red.

Take a look at the map on the left. As a general rule of thumb, red wines from the villages and regions on the left primarily use the Cabernet Sauvignon grape and on the right, the Merlot.

In all of Bordeaux, there are some 42,000 acres of Cabernet Sauvignon, 79,000 acres of Merlot, and 24,000 acres of Cabernet Franc.

The major shippers of regional wines from Bordeaux are:
Barton & Guestier (B & G)
Cordier
Dourthe Kressmann
Eschenauer
Sichel
Yvon Mau
Domaines Prats
Domaines Barons de Rothschild
CVBG
Ets J-P Moueix
La Basonnie
Borie-Manoux
Dulong

The "bread and butter" wines of Bordeaux are the regional and proprietary wines. These wines are meant to be consumed within two to three years after the harvest.

Examples of proprietary wines you may be familiar with:
Lauretan
Maître d'Estournel
Lacour Pavillon
Mouton-Cadet
Baron Philippe
Saint Jovian
Michel Lynch

Now's the time to start memorizing. In Bordeaux there are more than 9,000 individual châteaus!

Which grape varieties are grown in Bordeaux?

The three major grapes are:

Merlot   **Cabernet Sauvignon**   **Cabernet Franc**

Unlike in Burgundy, where the winemaker must use 100 percent Pinot Noir to make most red wines (100 percent Gamay for Beaujolais), the red wines in Bordeaux are almost always made from a blend of grapes.

What are the different quality levels of Bordeaux wine?

Bordeaux—This is the lowest level of A.O.C. wine in Bordeaux—wines that are nice, inexpensive, and consistent "drinking" wines. These are sometimes known as "proprietary" wines—wines known by what you could almost call a brand name, such as Mouton-Cadet, rather than by the particular region or vineyard. These are usually the least expensive A.O.C. wines in Bordeaux.

Bordeaux + Region—Regional wines come from a defined area. Only grapes and wines made in that certain area can be called by its regional name. For example, Médoc and St-Émilion. These wines are more expensive than than those labelled simply as Bordeaux.

Bordeaux + Region + Château—Château wines are the products of individual vineyards. There are more than 9,000 châteaux in Bordeaux.

As far back as 1855, Bordeaux officially classified the quality levels of some of its châteaux. Hundreds have been officially recognized for their quality. In the Médoc, for example, the 61 highest-level châteaux are called *Grand Cru Classé*. There are more than 240 chateaus in the Médoc that are entitled to be called *Cru Bourgeois*, a step below *Grand Cru Classé*. Other areas, such as St-Émilion and Graves, have their own classification systems.

Château wines are usually considered the best quality wines from Bordeaux. They are the most expensive wines, with some examples of the best known of the Grand Cru Classé commanding the highest wine prices in the world.

Bordeaux (proprietary)	**Regional**	**Château**

What's a château?

When most people think of a château, they picture a grandiose home filled with Persian rugs and valuable antiques and surrounded by rolling hills of vineyards. Well, I'm sorry to shatter your dreams, but most châteaus are not like that at all. Yes, a château could be a mansion on a large estate, but it could also be a modest home with a two-car garage.

How do I know if the wine I buy was really bottled at the château?

These wines will bear a special mark on the label. Look for the words *Mis en bouteille au château* to see if your wine was château-bottled.

MIS EN BOUTEILLE AU CHATEAU

GRAND VIN
DE
CHATEAU LATOUR
PREMIER GRAND CRU CLASSE

PAUILLAC

75 CL

PRODUCE OF FRANCE

DÉPOSÉ   APPELLATION PAUILLAC CONTROLÉE

Let's take a closer look at the châteaus. One fact I've learned from my years of teaching wine is that no one wants to memorize the names of thousands of châteaus, so I'll shorten the list by starting with the most important classification in Bordeaux.

MÉDOC

When and how were the château wines classified?

More than 140 years ago in the Médoc region of Bordeaux, a wine classification was established. Brokers from the wine industry were asked in 1855 to rate the top Médoc wines according to price, which at that time was directly related to quality. (After all, don't we class everything, from cars to restaurants?) The brokers agreed, provided the classification would never become official. *Voilà!* The Official Classification of 1855!

According to French law, a château is a house attached to a vineyard having a specific number of acres, as well as having winemaking and storage facilities on the property. A wine may not be called a château wine unless it meets these criteria. The terms "domaine," "clos," and "cru" are also used.

GRAND CRU CLASSÉ

CHATEAU LA LAGUNE
HAUT·MÉDOC
APPELLATION HAUT·MÉDOC CONTROLÉE

SOCIÉTÉ CIVILE AGRICOLE DU CHATEAU LA LAGUNE
PROPRIÉTAIRE A LUDON (GIRONDE) FRANCE

MIS EN BOUTEILLE AU CHATEAU

97

The Official (1855) Classification of the Great Red Wines of Bordeaux

THE MÉDOC

One of the top five châteaus rated in the classification is not owned by a Frenchman: Château Haut-Brion is owned by the Dillons, an American family.

FIRST GROWTHS—PREMIERS CRUS (5)

Vineyard	Commune
Château Lafite–Rothschild	Pauillac
Château Latour	Pauillac
Château Margaux	Margaux
Château Haut-Brion	Pessac (Graves)
Château Mouton-Rothschild	Pauillac

SECOND GROWTHS—DEUXIÈMES CRUS (14)

Vineyard	Commune
Château Rausan-Ségla	Margaux
Château Rausan Gassies	Margaux
Château Léoville–Las Cases	St-Julien
Château Léoville-Poyferré	St-Julien
Château Léoville-Barton	St-Julien
Château Durfort-Vivens	Margaux
Château Lascombes	Margaux
Château Gruaud-Larose	St-Julien
Château Brane-Cantenac	Cantenac-Margaux
Château Pichon-Longueville—Baron	Pauillac
Château Pichon-Longueville-Lalande	Pauillac
Château Ducru-Beaucaillou	St-Julien
Château Cos d'Estournel	St-Estèphe
Château Montrose	St-Estèphe

THIRD GROWTHS-TROISIÈMES CRUS (14)

Vineyard	Commune
Château Giscours	Labarde
Château Kirwan	Cantenac-Margaux
Château d'Issan	Cantenac-Margaux
Château Lagrange	St-Julien
Château Langoa-Barton	St-Julien
Château Malescot-St-Exupéry	Margaux
Château Cantenac-Brown	Cantenac-Margaux
Château Palmer	Cantenac-Margaux
Château La Lagune	Ludon
Château Desmirail	Margaux
Château Calon-Ségur	St-Estèphe
Château Ferrière	Margaux
Château Marquis d'Alesme-Becker	Margaux
Château Boyd-Cantenac	Margaux

MIS EN BOUTEILLE AU CHATEAU

GRAND CRU CLASSÉ EN 1855

COS D'ESTOURNEL

SAINT-ESTEPHE
APPELLATION SAINT-ESTEPHE CONTROLEE

DOMAINES PRATS S.A. SAINT-ESTEPHE FRANCE

RED BORDEAUX WINE
750 ml
Imported by KOBRAND CORPORATION NEW YORK, N.Y.
SOLE U.S. IMPORTERS
PRODUCE OF FRANCE
ALC. BY VOL. 13 %

PRODUCE OF FRANCE

Château Giscours
GRAND CRU CLASSÉ EN 1855
MARGAUX

APPELLATION MARGAUX CONTRÔLÉE
MIS EN BOUTEILLE AU CHATEAU

750 ml   12,5 % vol
PAR S.A. DU CHATEAU GISCOURS A LABARDE 33460 MARGAUX - FRANCE
Fermière du G.F.A. du château Giscours, Nicolas TARI, GRT

FOURTH GROWTHS-QUATRIÈMES CRUS (10)

Vineyard	Commune
Château St-Pierre	St-Julien
Château Branaire-Ducru	St-Julien
Château Talbot	St-Julien
Château Duhart-Milon-Rothschild	Pauillac
Château Pouget	Cantenac-Margaux
Château La Tour-Carnet	St-Laurent
Château Lafon-Rochet	St-Estèphe
Château Beychevelle	St-Julien
Château Prieuré-Lichine	Cantenac-Margaux
Château Marquis de Terme	Margaux

FIFTH GROWTHS-CINQUIÈMES CRUS (18)

Vineyard	Commune
Château Pontet-Canet	Pauillac
Château Batailley	Pauillac
Château Grand-Puy-Lacoste	Pauillac
Château Grand-Puy-Ducasse	Pauillac
Château Haut-Batailley	Pauillac
Château Lynch-Bages	Pauillac
Château Lynch-Moussas	Pauillac
Château Dauzac	Labarde
Château d' Armailhac (called Château Mouton-Baron-Philippe from 1956 to 1988)	Pauillac
Château du Tertre	Arsac
Château Haut-Bages-Libéral	Pauillac
Château Pédesclaux	Pauillac
Château Belgrave	St-Laurent
Château Camensac	St-Laurent
Château Cos Labory	St-Estèphe
Château Clerc-Milon	Pauillac
Château Croizet Bages	Pauillac
Château Cantemerle	Macau

Don't be misled by the term "growth." It might make the concept easier to understand if you substitute the word "classification." Instead of saying a wine is "first growth," you could say, "first classification."

"The classified growths are divided in five classes and the price difference from one class to another is about 12%" — Traité Sur Les Vins du Médoc. William Frank, 1855

The only château included in the 1855 classification that was not a part of the Médoc was Château Haut-Brion of Graves. This château was so famous at the time that the wine brokers had no choice but to include it.

"For a given vintage there is quite a consistent ratio between the prices of the different classes, which is of considerable help to the trade. So a fifth growth would always sell at about half the price of a second. The thirds and fourths would get prices halfway between the seconds and the fifths. The first growths are getting about 25% over the second growths."— Bordeaux et Ses Vins, Ch. Cocks, 1868

Why weren't the wines of St-Émilion and Pomerol classed with the wines of the Médoc in 1855?

I compare this situation to the hotel classification that was done in the mid-1970s in New York City. The best hotels located on the West Side were never listed, since that area was considered not "chic" enough to merit listing. It's the same with wine classification. St-Émilion and Pomerol were simply not "chic" enough; these two areas were considered to be out of touch with the rest of the Bordeaux wine world.

Is the 1855 classification still in use today?

Every wine person knows about the 1855 classification, but much has changed since then. Some vineyards have doubled or tripled their production by buying up their neighbor's land, which is permitted by law. In some well-known "first-growth" vineyards, such as Château Margaux, the quality of the wine degenerated for a while when the family that owned the château wasn't putting enough money and time into the vineyard. In 1977, Château Margaux was sold to a Greek-French family (named Mentzelopoulos) for $16 million, and since then the quality of the wine has come back up to its "first-growth" standards.

Château Gloria, in the commune of St-Julien, is an example of a vineyard that didn't exist at the time of the 1855 classification. The late mayor of St-Julien, Henri Martin, bought many parcels of "second-growth" vineyards. As a result, he produced top-quality wine that is not included in the 1855 classification. It's also important to consider the techniques used to make wine today. They're a lot different from those used in 1855. Once again, the outcome is better wine. As you can see, some of the châteaus listed in the 1855 classification deserve a lesser ranking, while others deserve a better one.

That said, however, I can also say that, in general, I believe, even though this classification was done 140 years ago, in most cases it is still a very valid classification.

On the 1945 Mouton-Rothschild bottle, there is a big "V" that stands for Victory and the end of World War II. Each year thereafter, Philippe de Rothschild asked a different artist to design his labels, a tradition continued by the Baroness Phillippine, his daughter. Some of the most famous artists in the world have agreed to have their work grace the Mouton label, among them:
Jean Cocteau—1947
Salvador Dali—1958
Henry Moore—1964
Joan Miró—1969
Marc Chagall—1970
Pablo Picasso—1973
Robert Motherwell—1974
Andy Warhol—1975
John Huston—1982
Saul Steinberg—1983
Keith Haring—1988
Francis Bacon—1990
Setsuko—1991 (the first woman)

Have there ever been any changes in the 1855 classification?

Yes, but only once, in 1973. Château Mouton-Rothschild was elevated from a "second-growth" to a "first-growth" vineyard. There's a little story behind that, which is told in the box below.

Exception to the Rule . . .

In 1920, when the Baron Philippe de Rothschild took over the family vineyard, he couldn't accept the fact that back in 1855 his château had been rated a "second growth." He thought it should have been classed a "first growth" from the beginning—and he fought to get to the top for some fifty years. While the Baron's wine was classified as a "second growth," his motto was:

> First, I cannot be.
> Second, I do not deign to be.
> Mouton, I am.

When his wine was elevated to a "first growth" in 1973, Rothschild had to stop using his old motto. He replaced it with a new one:

> First, I am.
> Second, I was.
> But Mouton does not change.

I've always found the 1855 classification to be a little cumbersome, so one day I sat down and drew up my own chart. I separated the classification into "growths" (first, second, third, etc.) and then I listed the communes (Pauillac, Margaux, St-Julien, and so on) and set down the number of distinctive vineyards in each one. My chart shows which communes of Bordeaux have the most "first growths"—all the way down to "fifth growths." It also shows which commune corners the market on *all* "growths." Since I was inspired to figure this out during baseball's World Series, I call my chart a "box score" of the 1855 classification.

A quick glance at my box score gives you some instant facts that may guide you when you want to buy a Bordeaux wine from Médoc.

Kevin Zraly's Box Score of the 1855 Classification

Commune	1st	2nd	3rd	4th	5th	Total
Margaux	1	5	10	3	2	21
Pauillac	3	2	0	1	12	18
St-Julien	0	5	2	4	0	11
St-Estèphe	0	2	1	1	1	5
St-Laurent	0	0	0	1	2	3
Haut-Médoc	0	0	1	0	1	2
Graves	1	0	0	0	0	1
	5	14	14	10	18	61

Total = 61 Châteaus

Tallying the score, Pauillac has three of the five "first growths." Margaux practically clean-sweeps the "third growths." In fact, Margaux is the overall winner, because it has the greatest number of classed vineyards in all of Médoc. Margaux is also the only area to have a château rated in each category. St-Julien has no "first" or "fifth growths," but is very strong in the "second" and "fourth."

POMEROL

This is the smallest of the top red-wine districts in Bordeaux. Pomerol produces only 15 percent as much wine as St-Émilion; as a result, Pomerol wines are relatively scarce. And if you do find them, they'll be expensive. Although no official classification exists, here's a list of some of the finest Pomerol wines on the market:

Château Pétrus

Château La Conseillante

Château Petit-Village

Château Trotanoy

Château l'Évangile

Vieux Château-Certan

Château Lapointe

Château Lafleur

Château La Fleur-Pétrus

Château Gazin

Château Beauregard

Château Nénin

Château Latour à Pomerol

The major grape used to produce wine in the Pomerol region is Merlot. Very little Cabernet Sauvignon is used in these wines.

The vineyard at Château Pétrus makes the most expensive wine of Bordeaux. It's planted with 95% Merlot.

It takes Château Pétrus one year to make as much wine as Gallo makes in six minutes.

The red wines of Pomerol tend to be softer, fruitier, and ready to be drunk sooner than the Médoc wines.

Some other appellations to look for in Bordeaux red wines:
Fronsac
Côtes de Blaye
Côtes de Bourg

ST-ÉMILION

This area produces about two-thirds as much wine as the entire Médoc, and it's one of the most beautiful villages in France (my own bias). The wines of St-Émilion were finally classified officially in 1955, one century after the Médoc classification. There are 11 "first growths" comparable to the "cru classé" wines of the Médoc, and some 70 grands crus classés.

The Eleven First Growths of St-Émilion (Premier Grande Crus Classés)

Château Ausone

Château Cheval Blanc

Château Beauséjour-Duffau

Château Bel-Air

Château Canon

Château Figeac

Château La Gaffelière

Château La Magdelaine

Château Pavie

Château Trottevieille

Château Clos Fourtet

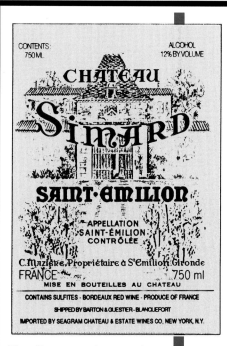

The Graves region produces 60% red wine, 40% white wine.

In 1987, a communal appellation was established to create a higher-level appellation in the Graves region. It's called Pessac-Léognan (for both reds and whites).

About vintages, the late Alexis Lichine, a noted wine expert, said: "Great vintages take time to mature. Lesser wines mature faster than the greater ones. . . Patience is needed for great vintages, hence the usefulness and enjoyment of lesser vintages." He summed it up: "Often vintages which have a poorer rating—if young—will give a greater enjoyment than a better-rated vintage—if young."

Important "grands crus classés" and other St-Émilion Wines Available in the U.S.:

Château L'Angélus

Château Canon-La Gaffelière

Château La Tour-Figeac

Château Trimoulet

Château Dassault

Château Simard

Château Monbousquet

Clos des Jacobins

GRAVES (PESSAC-LÉOGNAN)

The most famous château—we have already seen it in the 1855 classification—is Château Haut-Brion. Other good red Graves classified in 1959 as grands crus classés are:

Château Bouscaut

Château Haut-Bailly

Château Carbonnieux

Domaine de Chevalier

Château de Fieuzal

Château Olivier

Château Malartic-Lagravière

Château La Tour-Martillac

Château Smith-Haut-Lafitte

Château Pape-Clément

Château La Mission-Haut-Brion

Château La Tour-Haut-Brion

On Drinking the Wines of Bordeaux

The French drink their Bordeaux wines young, being afraid that a Socialist government will take it away from them.

The English drink their Bordeaux wines very old, because they like to take their friends down to their wine cellars with the cobwebs and the dust to show off their old bottles.

And the Americans drink their Bordeaux exactly when they are ready to be drunk, because they don't know any better.

—*Author Unknown*

Now that you know all the greatest red wines of Bordeaux, let me take you a step further and show you some of the best vintages.

The 1980s Were Unquestionably the Best Decade Ever for the Wines of Bordeaux

	1960s	1970s	1980s	1990s
Great Wines	1961	1970	1981	1990
	1966	1975	1982	
		1978	1983	
			1985	
			1986	
			1988	
			1989	
Good Wines	1962	1971	1984	1991
	1964	1973	1987	1992
	1967	1976		1993
		1979		
Off Years	1960	1972	1980	
	1963	1974		
	1965	1977		
	1968			
	1969			

How do I buy a red Bordeaux?

One of the biggest misconceptions about Bordeaux wines is that they are all very expensive. In reality, there are more than 9,000 châteaus at all different price ranges.

First and foremost, ask yourself if you want to drink the wine now, or if you want to age the wine. A great château in a great vintage needs a *minimum* of 10 years to age. Going down a level from there, you need to understand that a cru bourgeois or petit château in a great vintage needs a minimum of 5 years to age. A regional wine can be consumed within 2 or 3 years of the vintage year, while a wine labelled simply *Appellation Bordeaux Contrôlée* is ready to drink as soon as it's released.

The next step is to be sure the vintage is correct for what you want. If you're looking for a wine you want to age, in order to be able to age it, you must look for a great vintage. If you want a wine that's ready to drink now and you want a greater château, you should choose a lesser vintage.

The good news: 1990 produced the largest crop ever in Bordeaux and it's considered to be an outstanding year for fine Bordeaux wines.

The bad news: In April 1991, a frost destroyed more than 50% of Bordeaux's grape harvest.

Château Larose-Trintaudon is the largest vineyard in the Médoc area, making nearly 90,000 cases of wine per year.

If you want a wine that's ready to drink now and you want a great vintage, you should look for a lesser château.

Another consideration in buying the red wines of Bordeaux is to remember that Bordeaux wines are a blend. Ask yourself if you're looking for a Merlot style of Bordeaux, such as St-Émilion or Pomerol, or if you're looking for a Cabernet style, such as Médoc or Graves, remembering that the Merlot is more accessible and easier to drink when young

What does cru bourgeois mean?

The crus bourgeois of the Médoc are châteaus that were originally classified in 1920, and not in the 1855 classification. In 1932 there were 444 properties listed, but by 1962 there were only 94 members. Today there are over 400, with 150 belonging to the syndicate. The last classification of crus bourgeois of the Médoc and Haut-Médoc was in 1978. Because of the great vintages of the 1980s, some of the best values in wine today are in the cru bourgeois classification.

The following is a partial list of crus bourgeois to look for:

Château d'Angludet
Château Les Ormes-de-Pez
Château Les Ormes-Sorbet
Château Phélan-Ségur
Château Coufran
Château Chasse-Spleen
Château Meyney

Château Sociando-Mallet
Château Fourcas-Hosten
Château Larose-Trintaudon
Château Greysac
Château Marbuzet
Château Haut-Marbuzet
Château Patache d'Aux
Château La Cardonne
Château Poujeaux

What separates a $10 red Bordeaux from a $40 red Bordeaux?

- The place where the grapes are grown.
- The age of the vines themselves (usually the older the vine, the better the wine).
- The yield of the vine (lower yield means higher quality).
- Winemaking technique (for example, how long the wine is aged in wood).
- The vintage.

Is it necessary to pay a tremendous sum of money to get a great-tasting red Bordeaux wine?

It's nice if you have it to spend, but sometimes you don't. The best way to get the most for your money is to use what I call the "petit château" method. For example: Let's say you like Château Lafite-Rothschild, but you can't afford it. Look at the region. It's from Pauillac. You have a choice here: Either you can buy a regional wine called "Pauillac," or a petit château from Pauillac, or you can find a grand cru classé château which is rated lower than Lafite. Go to the 1855 classification, to the "fifth growths" and look for other Pauillacs. They may not be one-fifth of the price, but they will cost considerably less than the Lafite.

Since I didn't memorize the 9,000 châteaus myself, when I go to my neighborhood retailer, I look at the shelf and find a château I've never heard of. If it's from Pauillac, from a good vintage, and it's $10, I buy it. My chances are good. Everything in wine is hedging your bets.

Here is a list of my favorite red Bordeaux wines for 1996:

Château Lafite-Rothschild
Château Margaux
Château Latour
Château Haut-Brion
Château Mouton-Rothschild
Château Léoville-Las-Cases
Château Léoville-Poyferré
Château Léoville-Barton
Château Gruaud-Larose

Château Pichon-Longueville-Lalande
Château Ducru-Beaucaillou
Château Cos d'Estournel
Château Giscours
Château Palmer
Château La Lagune
Château Calon-Ségur
Château Branaire-Ducru
Château Talbot
Château Duhart-Milon-Rothschild
Château Beychevelle
Château Prieuré-Lichine
Château Haut-Batailley
Château Grand-Puy-Lacoste
Château Lynch-Bages
Château d'Armailhac
Château Lascombes
Château Pétrus
Château Trotanoy
Château Ausone
Château Cheval Blanc
Château Figeac
Château Pavie
Château Clos Fourtet
Château La Mission-Haut-Brion
Château Carbonnieux
Château Pichon-Longueville-Baron
Château Canon
Château Haut-Bailly

What have been the trends in the red wines of Bordeaux over the last ten years?

These have been some of the most exciting times in this wine-producing area, with all the great vintages of the 1980s, and many of these wines are just starting reach peak drinkability. I think one of the biggest changes is not necessarily in the quality of the Bordeaux wines from the great châteaus, which has continued to be very consistent, but rather that the crus bourgeois and petits châteaux are getting a lot more recognition than ever before, and rightfully so. These wines represent some of the best values in wines today.

Years ago, because there were not so many great vintages in the 60s and 70s, all you could find on restaurant wine lists were the great châteaus. Now after the great decade of the 1980s, you'll be able to find some really great wines at reasonable prices—not necessarily the great châteaus, not necessarily the cru bourgeois châteaus, but in the simple regional wine or simple *Appellation Bordeaux Contrôlée*. These wines usually sell for under $10 a bottle, making them a great value for the money.

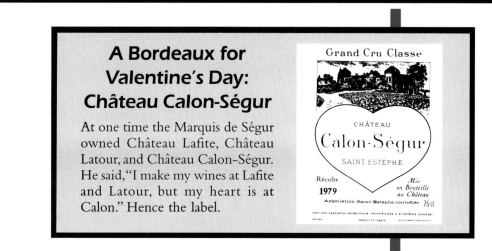

A Bordeaux for Valentine's Day: Château Calon-Ségur

At one time the Marquis de Ségur owned Château Lafite, Château Latour, and Château Calon-Ségur. He said, "I make my wines at Lafite and Latour, but my heart is at Calon." Hence the label.

Bordeaux still remains the number-one collectible wine in the world.

WINE AND food

Alain Querre (Château Monbousquet)—With St-Émilion or Pomerol wine, he recommends roast beef or grilled beef without sauce, seasoned with shallots, or in its own sauce. (A St-Émilion sauce is one of his favorites.) St-Estèphe goes well with lamb or lamprey eel, and red Graves is more enjoyable with fresh salmon.

Denise Lurton-Moulle (Château La Louvière, Château Bonnet)—With Château La Louvière rouge, roast leg of lamb or grilled duck breast.

Jean-Michel Cazes (Château Lynch-Bages, Château Haut-Bages-Averous, Château Les Ormes de Pez)—"For Bordeaux red, simple and classic is best! Red meat, such as beef and particularly lamb, as we love it in Pauillac. If you can grill the meat on vine cuttings, you are in heaven."

Alexis Lichine (Château Prieuré-Lichine)—Since fish are so good in the Atlantic region, he admitted having a definite preference for them. In the relaxed atmosphere of his dining room, he would have bass or any other Atlantic fish in a red wine sauce.

Bruno Prats (Château Cos d'Estournel)—He recommends simple food that is not too rich or served with too much sauce: leg of lamb in its own juice with a touch of garlic, veal with butter sauce, and roast duck with eggplant.

Antony Perrin (Château Carbonnieux)—For red Bordeaux, serve *magret de canard* (duck breast) with wild mushrooms, or Guinea hen with grapes *(pintade aux raisins).*

Had you dined at the Four Seasons restaurant in New York when it first opened in 1959, you could have had a 1918 Château Lafite-Rothschild for $18, or a 1934 Château Latour for $16. Or if those wines were a bit beyond your budget, you could have had a 1945 Château Cos d'Estournel for $9.50.

For further reading on Bordeaux wines: *Bordeaux,* by Robert Parker, and *Wines of Bordeaux,* by David Peppercorn, M.W., and Clive Coates, M.W.

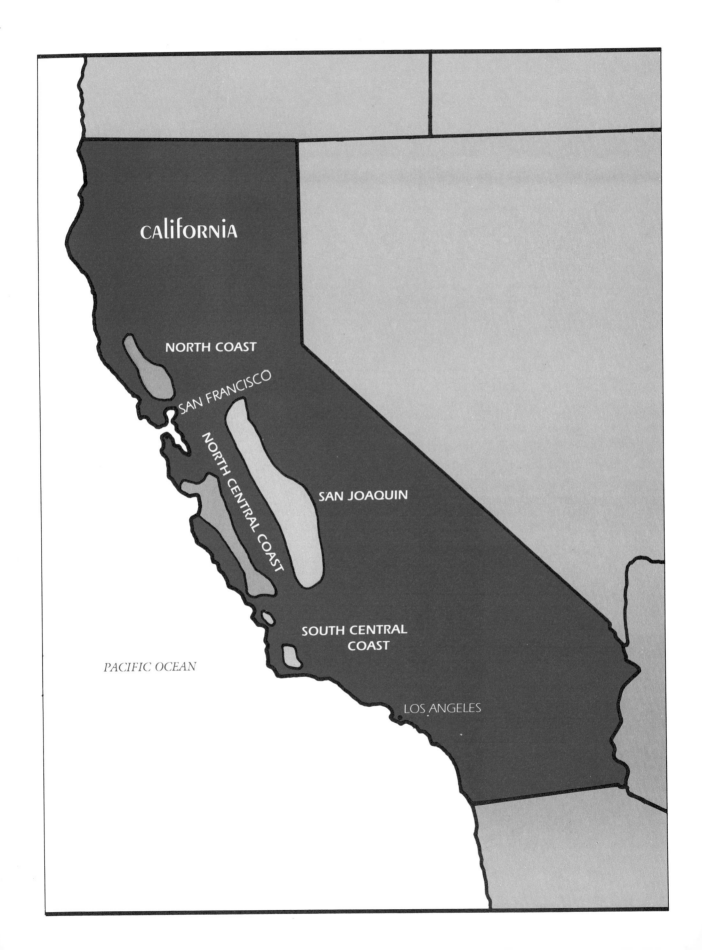

THe Red wiNes of califorNia

If I were to ask you what type of wine Americans prefer—red or white—what would you say? If you answered white, you are absolutely correct. But why am I bringing this up in the class on California red wine? Because 25 years ago there were more red grapes grown in California than white grapes.

That doesn't sound right, does it? Perhaps not, but there was a good reason for planting more red grapes than white ones, and it stemmed from American drinking habits. In 1960, Americans were consuming 83 percent red wines (including rosé); in 1970, 76 percent of the wines they consumed were red. If you were a vineyard owner in 1970, you would probably have planted red grapes.

Then, in the late 1970s a new trend began to develop. Americans began drinking more white wines than red wines. Ideally, you'd think the vineyard owner could uproot the red vines and replace them with white grapes to give the consumer what he wanted, but it's not that simple. As you already know, it takes three to five years from planting of the vines to the day the winemaker can produce wine from the grapes. That's the maturing process and its slow turnaround time.

Acreage in California: Currently there are 150,360 in red grapes, 176,310 in white grapes.

Red vs. White – Consumption in the United States

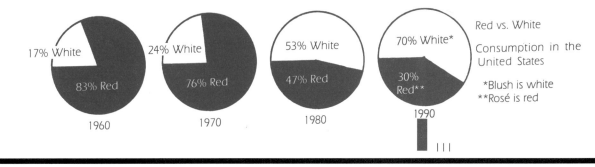

17% White
83% Red
1960

24% White
76% Red
1970

53% White
47% Red
1980

70% White*
30% Red**
1990

Red vs. White Consumption in the United States
*Blush is white
**Rosé is red

In 1994 red wine consumption had risen from 30% to 35%, with white wine consumption now at 65%.

At Windows on the World, we sold 75% white wine to 25% red wine.

On the average, one ounce of table wine = 18 calories.

Alcohol comparison: 5 oz. white wine = 12 oz. beer = 1.25 oz. liquor.

There has been a dramatic shift in the last few years in America's drinking habits. A trend that was going much more towards white wine has now seen an increase in red-wine consumption. Americans were drinking more white wine because they were changing their eating habits, switching from meat and potatoes to fish and vegetables and replacing cocktail parties with wine-and-cheese parties. Bars that never used to stock wine—or at least, nothing decent—began to carry an assortment of fine wines by the glass. But, as wine drinkers become more sophisticated, they often find more satisfaction and enjoyment in red wines.

But the power of television helped create a dramatic upturn in red-wine consumption. The TV series "Sixty Minutes" aired a report on a phenomenon known as the *French Paradox*—the fact that the French have a lower rate of heart disease than Americans, despite a diet that's higher in fat. Since the one thing the American diet lacks, in comparison to the French diet, is red wine, some researchers were looking for a link between the consumption of red wine and a decreased rate of heart disease. Not surprisingly, Americans significantly increased their purchases of red wines. This benefitted the California wine industry tremendously.

Drawing by Ed Fisher; © 1957 The New Yorker Magazine, Inc.

"You see? I've always told you California wines weren't so bad."

Red-Grape plantings

Look at the chart below to see how many acres of red grapes were planted in California by 1972, and how it increased in twenty years. Rapid expansion is characteristic of California's wine industry.

Total Acreage of Red-Wine Grapes Planted

1972 – 232,431 acres
1992 – 326,670 acres

Grape-by-Grape Comparison

Grape	1972	1982	1992
Cabernet Sauvignon	11,486	22,042	34,567
Pinot Noir	4,985	8,921	9,261
Zinfandel	23,786	28,045	34,142
Merlot	1,014	2,161	10,004

SUTTER HOME®

CALIFORNIA
WHITE ZINFANDEL
VINTED AND BOTTLED BY SUTTER HOME WINERY INC.
NAPA, CALIFORNIA 94589 BW 5525
ALCOHOL 9% BY VOLUME.

One of the hottest wines today in terms of popularity is white Zinfandel, which, at 16 million cases in 1992, not only far outsells red Zinfandel, but is also the largest-selling varietal wine in the United States.

What are the major red grapes winemakers use to make California reds?

Cabernet Sauvignon—Considered the most successful red *vinifera* grape in California, this grape yields some of the greatest red wines in the world. It is the predominant variety used in the finest red Bordeaux wines, such as Château Lafite-Rothschild and Château Latour. Almost all California Cabernets are dry, and depending upon the producer, they range in style from light to extremely full-bodied.

Best Bets for Cabernet Sauvignon

| 1984 | 1985 | 1986 | 1987 |
| 1990 | 1991 | 1992 | 1993 |

"Pinot Noir represents one of the biggest challenges to winemakers in California."— John Parducci

Pinot Noir—Known as the "headache" grape because of its fragile quality, Pinot Noir is difficult to grow and work with. The great grape of the Burgundy region of France—responsible for such famous wines as Pommard, Nuits-St-Georges, and Gevrey-Chambertin—is also one of the principal grapes in French Champagne. In California, many years of experimentation in finding the right location to plant the Pinot Noir and perfect the fermentation techniques have elevated some of the Pinot Noirs to the status of great wines. Pinot Noir is usually less tannic than Cabernet and matures more quickly, generally in two to five years. Because of all the extra expense involved in growing this grape, the best examples of Pinot Noirs from California may cost more than other varietals.

The Carneros district is one of the better places to grow Pinot Noir because of its cooler climate.

Zinfandel—The surprise grape of California, it was used to make "generic" or "jug" wines in the early years of California winemaking. Over the past 15 years, however, it has developed into one of the best red varietal grapes. It is unique among grapes grown in the United States in that its European origin is unknown. The only problem in choosing a Zinfandel wine is that so many different styles are made. Depending on the producer, the wines can range from a big, rich, intensely flavored style with substantial tannin, to very light, fruity wines.

Merlot—For many years Merlot was thought of as a grape only to be blended with Cabernet Sauvignon, because Merlot's tannins are softer and its texture more supple. Merlot is now achieving its own identity as a premium varietal. Of red grape varietals in California, Merlot has seen the fastest rate of new plantings in the last five years. It produces a soft, round wine, which generally does not need the same aging as a Cabernet Sauvignon. Because of these qualities, I expect it will be one of the top grape varieties in the next ten years, and it should be especially popular in restaurants, where its early maturation and the ease with which it can be matched with food should make it very popular.

Overheard at a wine shop in New York City from a customer buying a white Zinfandel: "You mean they make a red Zinfandel, too?"

There were only two acres of Merlot planted in all of California in 1960.

Ridge Winery may make six different Zinfandels and two different Cabernets every vintage.

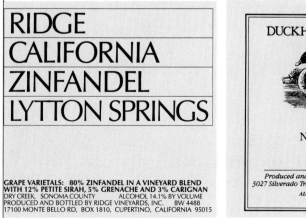

1972—The Baron Philippe de Rothschild said, "All American wines taste the same. They all taste like Coca-Cola."

1979—The Baron Philippe de Rothschild and Robert Mondavi formed a joint venture to produce a Bordeaux-style wine in the Napa Valley called Opus One.

When I buy a Cabernet, Zinfandel, Merlot, or Pinot Noir, how do I know which style I'm getting? Is the style of the wine indicated on the label?

Unless you just happen to be familiar with a particular vineyard's wine, you're stuck with trial-and-error tastings, because the winemaker doesn't usually indicate on the label whether a wine is ready to drink, or if it should be aged, or any other basic information. You're one step ahead, though, just by knowing that you'll find drastically different styles of the same wine.

To avoid any unpleasant surprises, I can't stress emphatically enough the importance of an educated wine retailer. One of the strongest recommendations I give—to a new wine drinker, especially—is to find the right retailer, one who understands wine and your taste.

Opus One

Amidst grand hoopla in the wine world, Robert Mondavi and the late Baron Philippe de Rothschild released Opus One. "It isn't Mouton and it isn't Mondavi," said Robert Mondavi. Opus One is a Bordeaux-style blend made from Cabernet Sauvignon, Merlot, and Cabernet Franc grapes. It was originally produced at the Robert Mondavi Winery in Napa Valley, but is now produced in its own winery.

The leading red varietal table wines produced in the United States in 1994:
1. Cabernet Sauvignon
2. Merlot
3. Zinfandel
4. Pinot Noir

1990 was a great year for all four.

California has had four great red-wine vintages in a row: 1990, 1991, 1992, and 1994.

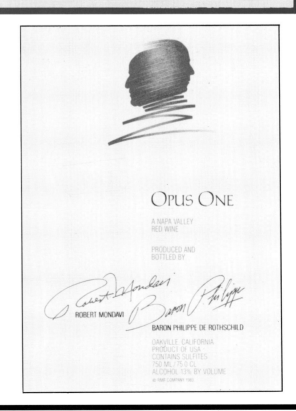

The best California wine I tasted in 1994 was Heitz Martha's Vineyard 1974.

What are Meritage wines?

Meritage® (which rhymes with "heritage") is its own category for red and white wines made in America from a blend of the classic Bordeaux wine-grape varieties. One of the main reasons this category was created was because many winemakers felt stifled by the minimum amount (75%) of a grape which must go into a bottle for it to be named for that variety. Some of the winemakers felt they could make a better wine with a blend of, say, 60% of the major grape and 40% of the secondary grape, so they created this category to give themselves the same freedom the Bordeaux winemakers have to make their wines.

For red wine, the varieties include Cabernet Sauvignon, Merlot, Cabernet Franc, Petit Verdot, and Malbec. For white wine, the varieties include Sauvignon Blanc and Sémillon.

Some examples of Meritage® wines of California:
Dominus (Christian Moueix)
Insignia (Phelps Vineyards)
Marlstone (Clos du Bois)
Rubicon (Niebaum Coppola Estate)
Opus One (Mondavi/ Rothschild)

In terms of vintage, how do I buy California wines? And how do I know when they're ready to drink?

One of the things I have noticed in the last ten years, not only tasting as many California wines as I have, but also tasting so many European wines, is that for some reason (and I don't know what that reason is) the California wines seem to be more accessible when young. This is one of the reasons California wines sell so well in retail stores and in restaurants. Still, some of the wines from the great California wineries will age just as well as their European counterparts.

What have been the trends in the red wines of California over the last ten years?

To best answer that question, we should go back even further to see where the trends have been going for the last thirty or so years. The 1960s were a decade of expansion and the development of what California wine would eventually become. The 1970s were a decade of growth in terms of the amount of wineries that came into being in California, and the corporations and individuals that became involved. The 1980s were the decade of experimentation for finding the right grapes to grow in the right locations and learning the right production and marketing techniques.

In the 1990s I foresee a "settling-down" of California, with the result of much higher quality wine. If you like California wines now, you're going to like them even more over the next ten years, because now that the winemakers have found their way, the days of experimentation are over. It's time to take everything they've learned and put that knowledge towards making the best quality wines they know how to make.

However, I don't expect Californians to give up experimentation altogether, but it will be with different grape varieties, such as the Viognier, Mourvèdre, Syrah, and Grenache varieties popular in the Rhône Valley in France, and the Sangiovese grapes from Italy. There will be a continuing trend towards diversity in California wines.

wine and food

Margrit Biever and Robert Mondavi—With Cabernet Sauvignon: lamb, wild game such as grouse and caribou. With Pinot Noir: pork loin, milder game such as domestic pheasant, coq au vin.

Antinori, the famous Italian winery, is part-owner of Napa Valley's Atlas Peak Winery, which has many acres planted to Sangiovese, the primary grape used to make Chianti.

Tom Jordan and Judy Jordan (Jordan Vineyard & Winery)—"Roast lamb is wonderful with the flavor and complexity of Cabernet Sauvignon. The wine also pairs nicely with sliced breast of duck, and grilled squab with wild mushrooms. For a cheese course with mature Cabernet, milder cheeses, such as young goat cheeses, St. André and Taleggio, are best so the subtle flavors of the wine can be enjoyed."

Margaret and Dan Duckhorn (Duckhorn Vineyards)—"With a young Merlot, we recommend lamb shanks with crispy polenta, or grilled duck with wild rice in Port sauce. With older Merlots at the end of the meal, we like to serve cambazzola cheese and warm walnuts."

Josh Jensen (Calera Wine Co.)—"Pinot Noir is so versatile, but I like it best with fowl of all sorts–chicken, turkey, duck, pheasant, and quail, preferably roasted or mesquite grilled. It's also great with fish such as salmon, tuna and snapper."

Louis Martini—With Cabernet Sauvignon: ripe Camembert cheese. With Pinot Noir: roast beef and good beef stew.

Sam J. Sebastiani (Viansa Winery)—With Cabernet Sauvignon: sliced tongue with blueberry sauce. With Pinot Noir: barbecued lamb with basting sauce of chopped chilies, olive oil, Pinot Noir, and honey. With Zinfandel: breast of veal stuffed with a combination of hot and mild Italian sausage, beef heart, toasted pine nuts, and chard.

Paul Draper (Ridge Vineyards)—With Zinfandel: a well-made risotto of Petaluma duck. With aged Cabernet Sauvignon: Moroccan lamb with figs.

Warren Winiarski (Stag's Leap Wine Cellars)—With Cabernet Sauvignon: lamb or veal with light sauces.

Janet Trefethen—With Cabernet Sauvignon: prime cut of well-aged grilled beef, also—believe it or not—with chocolate and chocolate-chip cookies. With Pinot Noir: roasted quail stuffed with peeled kiwi fruit in a Madeira sauce. Also with pork tenderloin in a fruity sauce.

For further reading on California wines I reccommend *A Wine Atlas of California,* by Bob Thompson, *Wines of California,* by James Halliday, and *Making Sense of California Wine,* by Matt Kramer. Cabernet lovers should read James Laube's *California's Great Cabernets.*

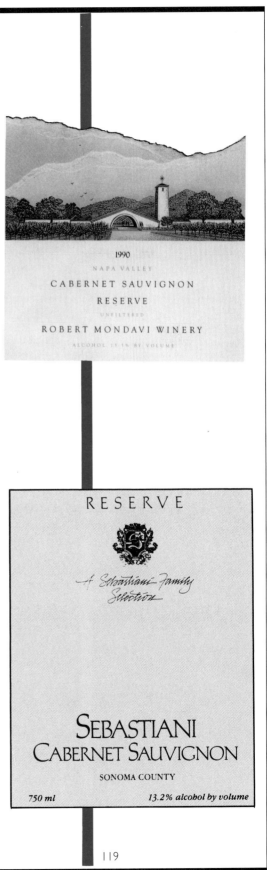

1990

NAPA VALLEY

CABERNET SAUVIGNON

RESERVE

UNFILTERED

ROBERT MONDAVI WINERY

ALCOHOL 13.5% BY VOLUME

RESERVE

A Sebastiani Family Selection

SEBASTIANI
CABERNET SAUVIGNON

SONOMA COUNTY

750 ml   13.2% alcohol by volume

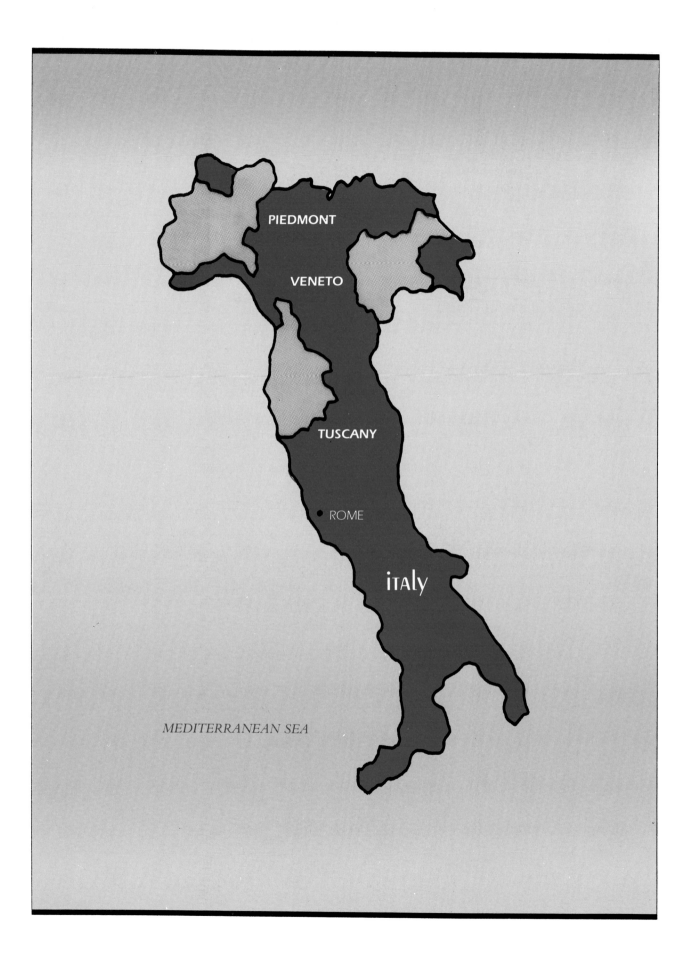

WINES of THE WORLD

THE RED WINES of ITALY

Italy is the world's biggest producer of wine. It has been producing wine for more than 3,000 years, and the vines grow *everywhere*. As one retailer of fine Italian wine says: "There is no country. Italy is one vast vineyard from north to south."

Italian wines are good for any occasion—from quaffing to serious tasting. Some of my favorite wines are Italian. In fact, 25 percent of my personal wine cellar is stocked with them.

There are more than 2,000 different wine labels, if you care to memorize them, 20 regions, and 93 provinces. But don't worry. If you want to know the basics of Italian wines, concentrate on the three regions listed below, and you'll be well on your way to having Italy in the palm of your hand.

Piedmont   **Tuscany**   **Veneto**

What are the major red-grape varieties in Italy?

Most of the best Italian red wines use Sangiovese grapes, in Tuscany, or Nebbiolo grapes, in Piedmont. There are several others, but these are the best.

How are Italian wines controlled?

As mentioned before, the Denominazione di Origine Controllata (abbreviated D.O.C.), the Italian equivalent of the French A.O.C., controls the production and labelling of the wine. Italy's D.O.C. laws went into effect in 1963.

There are more than 240 D.O.C. wines. They account for 12% to 15% of Italy's wine production.

Many wine producers in Italy are now making wines from Cabernet Sauvignon and Chardonnay.

The biggest difference between the A.O.C. of France and the D.O.C. of Italy is that the D.O.C. has aging requirements.

D.O.C. Laws

The D.O.C. governs:
1. The geographical limits of each region
2. The grape varieties that can be used
3. The percentage of each grape used
4. The maximum amount of wine that can be produced per acre
5. The minimum alcohol content of the wine
6. The aging requirements, such as how long a wine should spend in wood or bottle, for certain wines

D.O.C.G. wines from regions other than Tuscany and Piedmont include Taurasi from Campania, Albana di Romagna from Emilia-Romagna, and Torgiano Rosso Riserva from Umbria.

In Italy, vineyards aren't classified as they are in Bordeaux. There are neither grands crus nor premiers crus.

Before the D.O.C. laws were set up, some producers of Chianti established their own minimum standards that were quite strict. Their symbol was the black rooster, sometimes found on Chianti bottles.

How many of you, during your college days, bought a straw-covered bottle of Chianti to use as a candleholder?

Today you'll find that the best Chiantis are sold in Bordeaux-style bottles.

The Italian wine board took quality control even one step beyond the regular D.O.C., when they added the higher-ranking D.O.C.G. The "G" stands for *Garantita*, meaning that, through tasting-control boards, they absolutely guarantee the stylistic authenticity of a wine.

As of 1994, the wines from Piedmont and Tuscany that qualified for the D.O.C.G. were:

> **Vernaccia di San Gimignano**—from Tuscany
>
> **Chianti**—from Tuscany
>
> **Vino Nobile di Montepulciano**—from Tuscany
>
> **Carmignano**—from Tuscany
>
> **Brunello di Montalcino**—from Tuscany
>
> **Moscato d'Asti/Asti Spumante**—from Piedmont
>
> **Gattinara**—from Piedmont
>
> **Barbaresco**—from Piedmont
>
> **Barolo**—from Piedmont

Four of the Italian D.O.C.G. wines are from Piedmont, and five are from Tuscany. That tells you why these are two of the regions you should study.

TUSCANY—
THE HOME OF CHIANTI

Why did Chianti have such a bad image until recently?

One reason was the little straw–covered flasks (*fiaschi*) that the wine was bottled in—nice until restaurants hung the bottles from the ceiling next to the bar, along with the sausage and the provolone. So Chianti developed a bad image as a cheap little wine to be bought for $3 a jug.

My own feeling is that Chianti Classico Riserva is one of the best values in Italian wine today.

What are the different quality levels of Chianti?

Chianti—the first quality level (Cost: $)

Chianti Classico—from the inner district of Chianti (Cost: $$)

Chianti Classico Riserva—from a Classico area, aged for three
  years (Cost: $$$$)

How should I buy Chianti?

First of all, find the style of Chianti you like best. There is a considerable variation in Chianti styles. Second, always buy from a shipper or producer that you know—one with a good, reliable reputation. Some

quality Chianti producers are: Antinori, Badia a Coltibuono, Brolio, Frescobaldi, Melini, Monsanto, Nozzole, Ricasoli, Ruffino, and Villa Banfi.

Which grapes are used in Chianti?

According to updated D.O.C.G. requirements, winemakers are required to use at least 80% Sangiovese to produce Chianti. Besides decreasing the amount of white grapes that may be used, which tended to dilute the fruit and flavor of the wine, the D.O.C.G. is also encouraging the use of "non-traditional" grapes, such as Cabernet Sauvignon, by allowing an unprecedented 10% "optional grape." These changes, along with better winemaking techniques and better vineyard development, have all contributed to greatly improving Chianti's image over the last fifteen years.

Which other high-quality wines come from Tuscany?

Three of the greatest Italian red wines are Brunello di Montalcino, Vino Nobile di Montepulciano, and Carmignano. If you purchase the Brunello, keep in mind that it probably needs more aging (5 to 10 years) before it reaches peak drinkability. The best-known producers of Brunello are: Biondi-Santi (one of the most expensive wines in Italy), Barbi, Altesino, Il Poggione, and Col d'Orcia. Those of Vino Nobile are: Avignonesi, Boscarelli, Fassati and Poggio alla Sala. For Carmignano, look for Capezzana and Contini Bonacossi.

As in California, some Italian winemakers wanted to be able to experiment with grape varieties and blends beyond what was permitted by the D.O.C. regulations, so they decided to produce their own styles of wine. Among the better known of these proprietary Italians wines are Sassicaia, Tignanello, Ornellaia, Cabreo Il Borgo, and Solaia.

The top five wines imported to the U.S. from Italy are:
1. Riunite "Classics"
2. Bolla
3. Folonari
4. Canei
5. Cella
The above wines equal 40% of all imported table wine in the U.S.

It is said that when you begin drinking Italian wines, you start with the lighter-style Barbera and Dolcetto, move on to the fuller-bodied Barbaresco, until finally you can fully appreciate a Barolo. As the late vintner Renato Ratti said, "Barolo is the wine of arrival."

Piedmont's production:
90% red
9% spumante (sparkling white)
1% white

Two-thirds of all Italian wines are red.

Of all Italian D.O.C. wines, 60% are red.

piedmont—the big reds

The greatest variety of fine red wines is produced in Piedmont. Two of the best D.O.C.G. wines come from this region in northwest Italy: Barolo and Barbaresco.

The grapes of Piedmont

Barbera—Côtes du Rhône style

Dolcetto—Beaujolais style

Nebbiolo—The best!

Barolo and Barbaresco, the "heavyweight" wines from Piedmont, are made from the Nebbiolo variety. These wines have the fullest style and a high alcoholic content. Be careful when you try to match young vintages of these wines with your dinner; they may overpower the food.

Barolo vs. Barbaresco

BAROLO	BARBARESCO
Nebbiolo grape	Nebbiolo grape
Minimum 13% alcohol	Minimum 12.5% alcohol
More complex flavor, more body	Lighter; less body than Barolo
Must be aged at least three years (two in wood)	Requires two years of aging (one in wood)
"Riserva" = five years of aging	"Riserva" = four years of aging

What have been the trends in the red wines of Italy over the last ten years?

Going back a little further, we can see that as recently as twenty years ago Italian wine was made to be consumed at home, and not for the export market. As one wine producer commented, "They didn't drink the wine, they *ate* the wine." To the Italians, wine was an everyday thing. They didn't scrutinize a label, but only looked to see if the wine was red, white or rosé.

But, over the last twenty years, winemaking became more of a business, and the Italian winemakers' philosophy has changed considerably from making casual-drinking wines to much better-made wines that are also much more marketable around the world. They've accomplished this by using modern technology, modern vinification procedures, and updated vineyard management as a basis for experimentation. Another area of major experimentation is with non-traditional grape varieties such as Chardonnay and Sauvignon Blanc. As a result the biggest news in the whole wine industry is the change in Italian wines over the last ten years. When I talk about experimentation, you must remember that this isn't California we're talking about, but Italy, with thousands of years of traditions that are being changed.

The prices of Italian wines have also increased tremendously over the last ten years, which may be good news for the Italian wine producers (in that it enhances the image of their wines), but it isn't such good news for consumers. Some of the wines from Italy have become among the most expensive wines in the world. That's not to say they're not worth it, but the pricing situation isn't the same as it was ten years ago.

My favorite producers of Piedmont wines are: Antonio Vallana, Bersano, Borgogno, Fontanafredda, Gaja, Pio Cesare, Prunotto, Renato Ratti, Ceretto, G. Conterno, B. Giacose, Marchesi di Gresy, and Marcarini.

Have Piedmont wines changed over the last ten years? Many have. The wines of the past were more tannic and difficult to appreciate, while many of the present-day wines are easier to drink when young.

Giuseppe Colla of Prunotto offers his "Best Bets" in the form of advice. His general rule: In a good vintage, set a Barbaresco aside for a minimum of four years before drinking. In the same situation, put away a Barolo for six years. However, in a great vintage year, lay down a Barbaresco for six years and a Barolo for eight years. As they say, "Patience is a virtue"— especially with wine.

Best Bets for Tuscany

1982   1985   1988   1990   1993

Best Bets for Piedmont

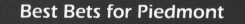

1982   1985   1988   1989   1990

VENETO—THE HOME OF SOAVE

This is one of Italy's largest wine-producing regions. Even if you don't recognize the name immediately, I'm sure you've had a Veronese wine at one time or another. They are Valpolicella, Bardolino, and Soave. All three are very consistent, easy to drink, and ready to be consumed whenever you buy them. They don't fit into the category of a Brunello di Montalcino or a Barolo, but they're very good table wines and they're within everyone's budget.

What's Amarone?

Amarone is a type of Valpolicella wine made by a special process in the Veneto region. Only the ripest grapes from the top of each bunch are used. After picking, they're left to "raisinate" (dry and shrivel) on straw mats. Does this sound familiar to you? It should, because this is similar to the process used to make German Trockenbeerenauslese and French Sauternes. One difference is that with Amarone, the winemaker ferments most of the sugar, bringing the alcohol content to 14–16 percent.

iTALiAN WhiTES

I am often asked why I don't teach a class on Italian white wines. The answer is quite simple. Take a look at the most popular white wines: Soave, Frascati, Pinot Grigio, Orvieto, and Verdicchio, among others. Every one of them retails for less than $10. The Italians just don't put the same effort into most of their white wines as they put into their reds—in terms of style or complexity—and they are the first to admit it.

For a new experience with Italian whites, try Gavi from Piedmont, and wines from the Friuli region.

How Italian Wines Are Named

Grape	Village or District	Proprietary
Barbera	Chianti	Rubesco
Nebbiolo	Barolo	Tignanello
Trebbiano	Barbaresco	
	Soave	

wine and food

In Italy, the wine is made to go with the food. No meal is served without wine. Take it from the experts:

The following food-and-wine suggestions are based on what some of the Italian wine producers enjoy eating with their wine. You don't have to take their word for it. Get yourself a bottle of wine, a tasty dish, and *mangia!*

Ambrogio Folonari (Ruffino)—He enjoys Chianti with prosciutto, chicken, pasta, and of course, pizza. When it comes to a Chianti Classico Riserva, Dr. Folonari prefers a hearty prime-rib dinner or a steak.

Ezio Rivella (Villa Banfi)—He says that Chianti is good with all meat dishes, but he saves the Brunello for "stronger" dishes, such as steak, wild boar, pheasant, and other game.

Angelo Gaja—He has Barbaresco with meat and veal, and also with mature cheeses that are "not too strong," such as Emmenthaler and Fontina. Mr. Gaja advises against Parmesan and goat cheese when you have a Barbaresco.

Giuseppe Colla (Prunotto)—Mr. Colla says light-style Dolcetto goes well with all first courses and all white meat—chicken and veal especially. He prefers not to have Dolcetto with fish. The wine doesn't stand up well to spicy sauce, but it's great with tomato sauce and pasta.

An interesting trend in Italy: Beer consumption is increasing, while wine consumption is decreasing.

In the last five or six years, Italians have become more weight- and health-conscious, so they're changing their eating habits. As a result, the long lunch hour is a thing of the past. Yes, all good things must come to an end.

"Piedmontese wines show better with food than in a tasting."   —Angelo Gaja

"When you're having Italian wines, you must not taste the wine alone. You must have them with food."
—Giuseppe Colla
of Prunotto

Renato Ratti—The late Mr. Ratti once told us that both Barbera and Dolcetto are good with chicken and lighter foods. However, Barolo and Barbaresco need to be served with heavier dishes to match their own body. Mr. Ratti also suggested:

- –a roast in its natural sauce or better yet, try *Brasato al Barolo*— cooked with Barolo
- –meat cooked with wine
- –pheasant, duck, wild rabbit
- –cheeses
- –for a special dish, try *risotto al Barolo* (rice cooked with Barolo wine)

Mr. Ratti said that Italians even serve wine with dessert—his favorite was strawberries or peaches with Dolcetto wine. The dryness in the wine contrasted with the natural sweetness of the fruit makes for a taste sensation!

Lorenza de'Medici (Badia a Coltibuono)—Since Tuscan cooking is very simple, this winery owner recommends an assortment of simple foods. She prefers herbs to heavy sauces. With young Chianti, she suggests roast chicken, squab, or pasta with meat sauce. To complement an older Chianti, she recommends a wide pasta with:

- –braised meat in Chianti
- –pheasant or other game
- –wild boar
- –roast beef

Piero Antinori (Antinori)—Mr. Antinori enjoys Chianti with the grilled foods for which Tuscany is famous, especially its *bistecca alla Fiorentina* (beefsteak). He suggests poultry and even hamburgers as other tasty possibilities.
For Chianti Classico Riserva, Mr. Antinori enjoys having the best of the vintages with wild boar and fine aged Parmesan cheese. He says the wine is a perfect match for roast beef, roast turkey, lamb, or veal.

For further reading on Italian wine: *The Pocket Guide to Italian Wines* and *Wine Atlas of Italy*, both by Burton Anderson; and *Italian Wine*, by Victor Hazan.

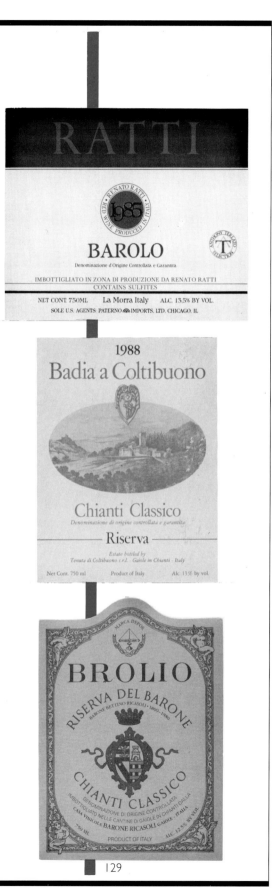

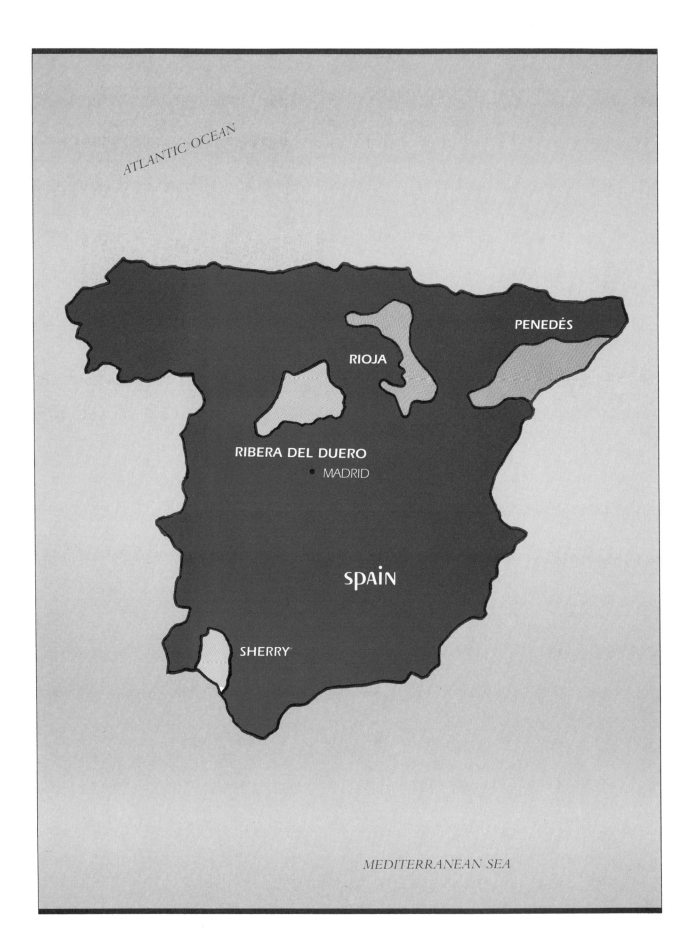

ATLANTIC OCEAN

PENEDÉS

RIOJA

RIBERA DEL DUERO

• MADRID

SPAIN

SHERRY

MEDITERRANEAN SEA

spain

The main winemaking regions in Spain are:

Rioja

Penedés

Ribera del Duero

Sherry

We'll put aside the region of Sherry for now, since you'll become a Sherry expert in the next chapter. Let's start with Rioja, which is located in northern Spain, very near the French border.

In fact, it's less than a five-hour drive to Bordeaux from Rioja, so it's no coincidence that Rioja wines often have a Bordeaux style. Back in the 1800s, many Bordeaux wine producers brought their expertise to this region.

Marqués de Cáceres is owned by a Spaniard, who also owns Château Camensac, a 5th-growth Bordeaux.

Why would a Frenchman leave his château in Bordeaux to go to a Spanish bodega in Rioja?

I'm glad you asked. It so happens that Frenchmen did travel from Bordeaux to Rioja at one point in history. Do you remember Phylloxera? (See the introductory chapter *Prelude to Wine.*) It's a plant louse that at one time killed nearly all the European vines and almost wiped out the Bordeaux wine industry.

Phylloxera started in the north and moved south. I'm not kidding when I say this, but the Phylloxera had trouble getting over the Pyrenees. Phylloxera destroyed all of the vines of Bordeaux first. Some of the Bordeaux vineyard owners decided to establish vineyards and wineries in the Rioja district. It was a logical place for them to go because of the similar climate and growing conditions. The influence of the Bordelaise is sometimes apparent even in today's Rioja wines.

Which grapes are used in Rioja wines?

The major grapes used in Rioja wine are:

Tempranillo

Garnacha (related to the Grenache of the Rhône Valley)

These grapes are blended to give Rioja wines their distinctive taste. If you do see a vintage on a Rioja label, you'll find it next to the word *cosecha*, which means harvest.

The Viura is the most used grape in White Rioja.

131

Spain's Wine Renaissance

Spain is the world's third-largest producer of wine, behind France and Italy. Spain has more land dedicated to vines than any other country: 4.5 million acres!

Spain is also a country with a rich winemaking tradition. Many types of wine are produced: Cava (*méthode champenoise* sparkling wines) are produced in the Penedés region not far from Barcelona. Red wines and rosés are produced throughout the entire country. Fortified wines are produced mainly in the south. The best-known region for such wines is obviously Jerez (Sherry).

A 20th-century renaissance extends nationwide to Spain's wine industry, where tremendous investments have been made throughout the country in viticulture and winemaking equipment. In Rioja alone, the number of wineries has increased from 42 to 149 since 1982.

Have Rioja wines changed in style over the last 20 years?

Look for the 1982, 1985, 1988, 1989 and 1990 vintages.

Yes, without a doubt. As has been the case in Italy, modern technology and new viticultural procedures have made for much better wines, many of which merit long-term aging. In particular, wines that in the past were aged for a long time in wood—both reds and whites—are now being taken out of the wood sooner and placed in the bottle to retain the fruit flavor..

Why are Rioja wines so easy to understand?

All you need to know when buying a Rioja wine is the style (level) and the reputation of the Rioja winemaker/shipper. The grape varieties are not found on the wine labels, and there's no classification to be memorized. The three major levels of Rioja wines are:

1. Crianza ($)—one year in oak barrels, one year in the bottle
2. Reserva ($$)—one year in oak barrels, two years in the bottle
3. Gran Reserva ($$$$)—two years in oak barrels, three years in the bottle

How would I know which Rioja wine to buy in the store?

You mean besides going with your preferred style and the reputation of the winemaker/shipper? You may also be familiar with a Rioja wine by its proprietary name. The following are some bodegas to look for, along with some of their better-known proprietary names:

Federico Paternina—Banda Azul

C.U.N.E.—Imperial, Viña Real

Bodegas Bilbainas—Brillante, Viña Pomal

Marqués de Cáceres

Marqués de Riscal

Bodegas Domecq-Marqués de Arienzo

Marqués de Murrieta

Ollara

Bodegas Riojanas

Bodegas Montecillo—Viña Cumbrero, Viña Monty

La Rioja Alta—Viña Alberdi, Viña Ardanza

The two other famous winegrowing regions in Spain are Penedés (outside Barcelona) and the Ribera del Duero (between Madrid and Rioja). The most famous wine of the Penedés region is the sparkling wine called "cava," of which the two best-known names in the United States are Codorniu and Freixenet. These are two of the biggest producers of bottle-fermented sparkling wine in the world, and one of the best features of these wines is their reasonable price. The Penedés region is also known for high-quality table wine. The major producer of this region (and synonymous with the quality of the area) is the Torres family. Their famous wine, Gran Coronas Black Label, is made with 100% Cabernet Sauvignon. The wines of Jean Leon are also prevalent.

The Ribera del Duero has been around since the 1800s (though it was officially delimited in 1982), but is now becoming quite prominent in the United States. It's considered to be the "new" area of Spain. One of the most expensive Spanish wines, called Vega Sicilia, is produced there. Another top wine, which is less expensive but more readily available, is called Pesquera.

Another up-and-coming area in Spain is called Rias Baixas, in the northwestern province of Galicia, producing some excellent white wines made with the Albariño grape. Delimited in 1988, Rias Baixas is the wettest and coolest of Spain's wine regions.

Ribera del Duero wines are made from the Tinto Fino grape, a close cousin of Rioja's Tempranillo. The laws also allow the use of Cabernet Sauvignon, Malbec, Merlot, and small amounts of a white grape called Albillo.

Further reading: *The Wines of Rioja*, by Hubrecht Duijker.

THE WINES OF AUSTRALIA

There are about 30 distinct winegrowing regions in Australia, with some 80 districts and subdistricts. Do you need to know them all? Probably not, but within Australia's six states, you should be familiar with the best districts in four states:

New South Wales (N.S.W.)
—Hunter Valley, Mudgee

South Australia (S.A.)
—Adelaide Hills, Barossa Valley, Clare, Coonawarra, Padthaway, Southern Vales (McLaren Vale)

Victoria (Vic.)
—Bendigo, Geelong, Great Western, Goulburn Valley, Milawa, Moonambel, Mornington Peninsula, Rutherglew, Yarra Valley

Western Australia (W.A.)
—Frankland, Lower Great Southern, Margaret River

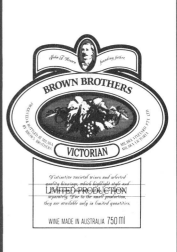

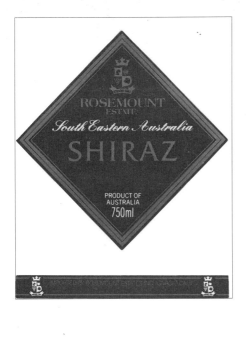

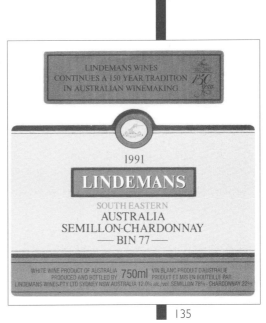

The Australian wine industry began in 1788 with the planting of Australia's first grapevines. In 1823, Gregory Blaxland won a silver medal for one of his red wines; in London in 1828 he won a gold medal for another wine, from fruit grown near Sydney.

Two-thirds of Australian wine grapes are white varieties. Although there are nearly 700 different wineries in the country, almost all of its production comes from only 65 of its biggest companies.

In the 1830s, vine cuttings from Château Haut Brion in Bordeaux were planted near Melbourne. In 1832, James Busby brought back Shiraz cuttings from Chapoutier in the Rhône Valley, which he planted in the Hunter Valley.

The 1990 vintage in Australia was the largest harvest ever, and one of the finest.

The wine industry is by no means new to Australia. In fact, many of Australia's leading wine companies were established more than 175 years ago. Lindeman's, Penfolds, Orlando, Henschke and Seppelt are just a few of the companies that were founded during the 19th century. They are now among Australia's largest, or most prestigious, companies, and they produce excellent wines.

Which grape varieties are grown in Australia?

Major red grape varieties are:

Shiraz (Hermitage)—The Syrah of the Rhône Valley in France. It produces big, robust, long-lived and full-bodied wines.

Cabernet Sauvignon—As in Bordeaux and California, it produces some of the best wines in the country. Always dry, and depending on the producer and the region, Cabernet yields wines that range in style from medium to extremely full-bodied. It is often blended with Shiraz.

Pinot Noir—The great grape of Burgundy. In many cooler districts of Victoria, South Australia and Western Australia, it is beginning to show signs of reaching quality levels similar to those of its famous brethren.

The main white grape varieties are:

Rhine Riesling—A variety also grown in Germany, Alsace and California (Johannisberg Riesling). It ranges in style from dry to sweet.

Sémillon—In France, this grape is blended with Sauvignon Blanc to make white Bordeaux. In Australia, where it is also known as "Hunter Riesling," it makes medium-style, dry wines, and is often blended with Chardonnay.

Chardonnay—As in Burgundy and California, Chardonnay makes dry, full-flavored wines, as well as being the base wine for sparkling wines.

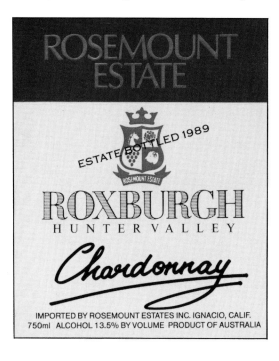

What kinds of wine are produced in Australia?

Most of the original vineyards planted in Australia were in quite warm, dry locations, and so Australia was originally known for producing big, robust, full-bodied red wines. Winemakers named their wines after their European counterparts (as was done in California); "Claret" and "Burgundy" indicated lighter and fuller red wines. "Riesling" meant a light, fruity white wine, while "White Burgundy" suggested a drier, medium-bodied white wine.

Today, Australia produces many different kinds of table wine, ranging from "German"-style whites to red varietal wines aged in small oak barrels. The best wines are those labelled with the grape varieties.

Among the most interesting winemaking practices of Australia are the white blends made from Chardonnay and Sémillon and the red blends made of Cabernet and Shiraz. Not only do these blends represent high quality at reasonable prices, but they are also "fun" wines.

How are wines labelled?

Though Australia has no national labelling requirements to match the A.O.C. laws of France, the states regulate labels that list varieties or regions. In this case, the label gives you a great deal of information, as in this example:

One of the most important pieces of information is the producer's name. In this case, the producer is Penfolds. If the grape variety is printed on the label, the wine must be made from at least 80% of that variety. In a blend listing the varieties, as above, the percentages of each must be shown. If the label specifies a particular wine-growing district (for example, Coonawarra), at least 80% of the wine must originate there. If a vintage is given, 95% of the wine must be of that vintage.

What about vintages?

While Australia's climate is generally not unlike that of California, one should not be tempted to generalize that there is the same constancy of vintage throughout the country. After all, Australian winegrowing regions extend across 3,000 miles. Still, in any given vintage, there will usually be several regions that produce excellent wine. As for value, the Australian dollar in 1995 was worth about 70% of our own, so Australian wines are an excellent buy.

My list of top Australian wineries includes Brown Brothers, Hardy's, Lindemans, Orlando, Michelton, Yolumba, Rothbury, Penfolds, Petaluma, Rosemount, Wolf Blass, Henschke, and Mountadam.

"Cask" or "Bag-in-Box" are wine terms for bulk or "jug" wines. "Bin Numbers" are Australia's way of indicating style.

The vintage in Australia occurs in the first half of the year. The grapes are harvested from February to May. For any given vintage, Australia will have its wines approximately six months before Europe or America.

Best bets for red wines: 1986, 1987, 1990, 1991, 1992

Best bets for white wines: 1986, 1988, 1990, 1991

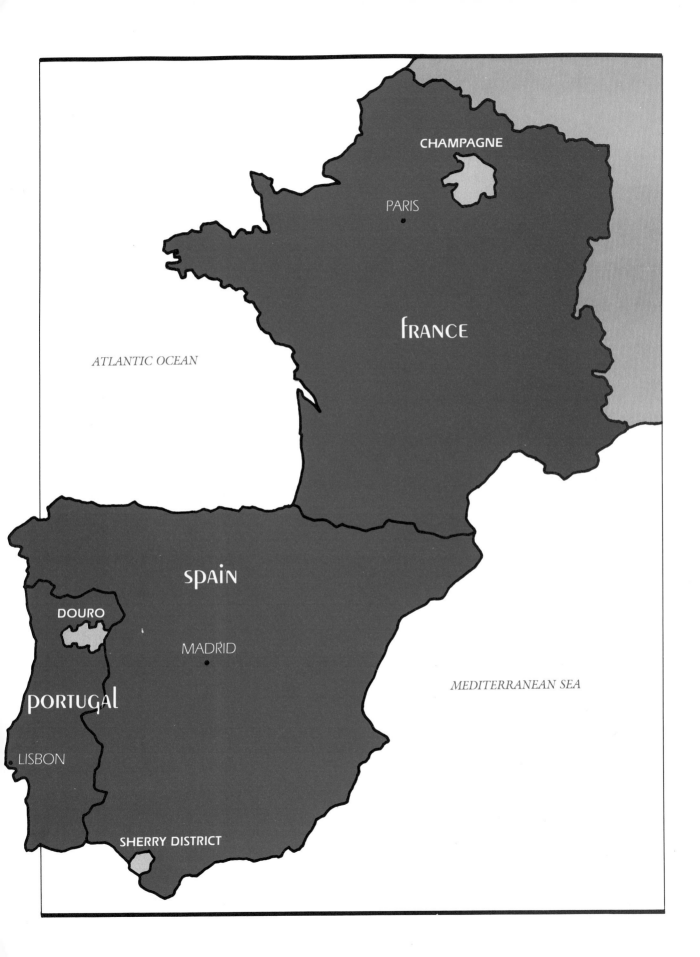

CHAMPAGNE

PARIS

FRANCE

france

ATLANTIC OCEAN

spain

DOURO

MADRID

MEDITERRANEAN SEA

portugal

LISBON

SHERRY DISTRICT

CHAMPAGNE, SHERRY, AND PORT

Now we're beginning our last class—the last chapter on the wine itself. This is where the course ends—on a happy note, I might add. What better way to celebrate than with Champagne?

Why do I group Champagne, Sherry, and Port together? Because as diverse as these wines are, the way the consumer will buy them is through the reputation and reliability of the shipper. Since these are all blended wines, the shipper is responsible for all phases of the production—you concern yourself with the house style. In Champagne, for example, Moët & Chandon is a well-known house; in Port, the house of Sandeman; and in Sherry, the house of Pedro Domecq.

The Champagne region covers about 85,000 acres, or 2.5% of French vineyards. Production is about 220 million bottles a year, which represents about 10% of world production of sparkling wines.

CHAMPAGNE

What's Champagne?

We all know that Champagne is a sparkling bubbly that everyone drinks on New Year's Eve. It's more than that. Champagne is a region in France—the country's northernmost winemaking region, to be exact—and it's an hour and a half northeast of Paris.

Why do I stress its northern location? Because this affects the taste of the wine. In the Champagne region, the growing season is shorter; thus, the grapes are picked with higher acidity than in most other regions, which is one of the reasons for Champagne's distinct taste. The Champagne region is divided into three main areas:

Valley of the Marne

Mountain of Reims

Côte des Blancs

To evaluate Champagne, look at the bubbles. The better wines have smaller bubbles and more of them. Also, with a good Champagne, the bubbles last longer.

Acidity in Champagne not only gives freshness to the wine, but is also important to its longevity.

139

The balance of the fruit and acidity, together with the bubbles (CO_2), are what make good Champagne.

"In victory you deserve it; in defeat you need it."
—Christian Pol Roger

Blanc de Blancs is white wine made from 100% white grapes—Chardonnay.

All Appellation Contrôlée sparkling wines made in France, including Champagne, must be made by the Méthode Champenoise.

About 20% of the sparkling wines made in the United States are made by the Méthode Champenoise.

Most Champagnes are fermented in stainless steel.

"Fermentation in barrels is absolutely out of date."
—Bertrand Mure, Ruinart

Wine presses are placed throughout the vineyards so the winemaker can press the red grapes immediately without extracting any of their color.

Over 80% of the Champagne produced is non-vintage. This means it's a blend of several years' harvests.

Until around 1850, all Champagne was sweet.

Three grapes can be used to produce Champagne:

Pinot Noir (red)—accounts for 37 percent of all grapes planted.

Pinot Meunier (red)—accounts for 37 percent of all grapes planted.

Chardonnay (white)—accounts for 26 percent of all grapes planted.

In France, only sparkling wines that come from the region of Champagne may be called "Champagne." Some American producers have borrowed the name "Champagne" to put on the label of their sparkling wines. These cannot and should not be compared with Champagne from France.

How's Champagne made?

Champagne is made by a process called the *Méthode Champenoise*, which is described below, step-by-step.

MÉTHODE CHAMPENOISE

Harvest—The normal harvest usually takes place in late September or early October.

Pressing the Grapes—Only two pressings of the grapes are permitted. The first pressing is called the *cuvée*, which goes into making the highest-quality Champagne. The second pressing, called the *taille*, usually goes into making non-vintage Champagnes.

Fermentation—All Champagnes undergo a first fermentation when the grape juice is converted into wine. Remember the formula: Sugar + Yeast = Alcohol + CO_2. The carbon dioxide dissipates. The first fermentation takes two to three weeks and produces still wines.

Blending—The most important step in Champagne production. The winemaker has to make many decisions here. Three of the more important ones are: (1) Which grapes to blend—how much Chardonnay, Pinot Noir, and Pinot Meunier? (2) From which vineyards should the grapes come? (3) Which years or vintages should be blended?

Liqueur de Tirage—After the blending process, the winemaker adds *Liqueur de Tirage*—a blend of sugar and yeast—which will begin the wine's second fermentation. At this point, the wine is placed in its permanent bottle with a temporary bottle cap.

Second Fermentation—During this fermentation, the carbon dioxide stays in the bottle. This is where the bubbles come from. The second fermentation also leaves natural sediments in the bottle. Now the problems begin. How do you get rid of the sediments without losing the carbon dioxide? Go on to the next steps.

Aging—The amount of time the wine spends aging on its sediments is one of the most important factors in determining the quality of the wine.

Riddling—The wine bottles are now placed in A-frame racks, necks down. The *remueur*, or riddler, goes through the racks of Champagne bottles and gives each bottle a slight turn while gradually tipping the bottle further downwards. After six to eight weeks, the bottle stands almost completely upside down, with the sediments resting in the neck of the bottle.

Dégorgement—The top of the bottle is dipped into a brine solution to freeze it, and then the temporary bottle cap is removed and out flies the frozen sediments, propelled by the carbon dioxide.

Dosage—A combination of wine and cane sugar is added to the bottle after dégorgement. At this point, the winemaker can determine whether he wants a sweeter or a drier Champagne.

Recorking—The wine is recorked with real cork instead of a bottle cap.

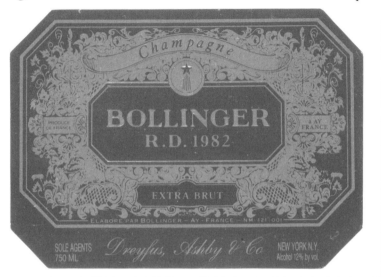

Non-vintage Champagne must be kept in the bottle for at least one year. Vintage Champagne cannot be sold until three years after the harvest. (In practice, most of the fine houses age non-vintage Champagne for three years, and vintage for five years.)

Champagne is put into heavy bottles to hold the pressurized wine. This is another reason why Champagne is more expensive than ordinary wine.

Two methods of making rosé Champagne: (1) add red wine; (2) leave the red grape skins in contact with the must for a short period of time.

Occasionally a Champagne will be labelled "extra brut," which is drier still than brut.

Dosage

The dosage determines whether the wine will be the driest style, brut, a sweet demi-sec, or any style in between. The following shows you the guidelines the winemaker uses when he adds the dosage.

Brut—driest
Extra dry—less dry
Sec—more sweet
Demi-sec—sweetest

Brut and extra-dry are the wines to serve as apéritifs, or throughout the meal. Sec and demi-sec are the wines to serve with desserts and wedding cake!

What accounts for the different styles of Champagne?

Going back to the three grapes we talked about that are used to make Champagne, the general rule is:

The more white grapes used in the blend, the lighter the style of the Champagne.

The more red grapes used in the blend, the fuller the style of the Champagne.

Also, some producers ferment their wines in wood. Bollinger ferments some, and Krug ferments all of their wines this way. This gives the Champagne fuller body and bouquet than those fermented in stainless steel.

How do I buy a good Champagne?

First, determine the style you prefer, whether full-bodied or light-bodied, a dry brut or a sweet demi-sec. Then make sure you buy your Champagne from a reliable shipper/producer. Each producer takes pride in its distinctive house style, and strives for a consistent blend, year after year. The following are some brands in national distribution to look for. While it is difficult to be precise, the designations generally conform to the style of the houses.

The top five Champagne houses in shipments to the United States in 1993: Moët & Chandon, G.H. Mumm, Perrier-Jouët, Veuve Clicquot, and Taittinger.

There are more than 100 Champagne houses in France and about 25–30 Champagnes available in the United States.

Champagne houses market about two-thirds of Champagne's wines, but they own less than 10% of the vineyards.

Light, delicate
A. Charbaut et Fils
Lanson

Light to Medium
Billecart-Salmon
Deutz
Laurent-Perrier
G.H. Mumm
Perrier-Jouët
Pommery
Ruinart Père & Fils
Taittinger

Medium
Charles Heidsieck
Moët & Chandon
Piper-Heidsieck
Pol Roger

Medium to Full
Henriot
Louis Roederer

Full, rich
Bollinger
Krug
Veuve Clicquot

What are the three major types of Champagne?

—**non-vintage**

—**vintage**

—**"prestige"**

Is every year a vintage year?

No, but the top vintages of the 1980s were 1982, 1983, 1988, and 1989. *Note:* These were vintage years for most Champagne houses. "Vintage" in Champagne is different from other wine regions, because each house makes its own determination on whether or not to declare a vintage year.

Why's there such a tremendous price difference between non-vintage and "prestige" Champagnes?

"Prestige" Champagnes usually meet the following requirements to be designated as such:

—Made from the best grapes of the highest-rated vineyards

—Made from the first pressing of the grapes

—Spent more time aging in the bottle than non–vintage Champagnes

—Made only in vintage years

—Made in small quantity, and the demand is high. Price is dictated largely by supply and demand.

Non-vintage Champagne is more typical of the house style than vintage Champagne.

Vintage Champagne must contain 100% of that vintage year's harvest.

Shippers don't always agree on the quality of the wines produced in any given vintage, so the years for vintage Champagnes vary from shipper to shipper. Each house usually declares a vintage three years out of each decade.

Dom Pérignon Champagne is aged 6 to 8 years before it is put on the market.

Now that we've gone through the different levels of Champagne, I'll let you in on a little secret. When I buy Champagne, I prefer non–vintage over both vintage and "prestige" Champagnes. That's what tastes best for me, and it's definitely the best value for the money.

When's Champagne ready to drink?

As soon as you buy it. You can keep the bottle for three to four years after you purchase it, but the wine won't improve. Champagne is something you shouldn't put away. So if you're still saving that Dom Pérignon that you received for your tenth wedding anniversary fifteen years ago, don't wait any longer to open it.

What's the correct way to open a bottle of Champagne?

Before we sip Champagne in class, I always take a few moments to show everyone how to open a bottle of Champagne properly. I do this for a good reason. Opening a bottle of Champagne can be dangerous, and I'm not kidding. I've always stressed this to all the servers and captains at Windows on the World. If you know the pounds per square inch that are under pressure in the bottle, you know what I'm talking about. It is especially important that the bottle be chilled before you open it.

Opening Champagne Correctly

1. Cut the foil around the top of the bottle.

2. Place your hand on top of the cork, never removing your hand until the cork is pulled out completely. (I know this may seem a bit awkward, but it's very important.)

3. Take off the wire.

4. Wrap a towel around the bottle for safety and spillage, "just in case."

5. Remove the cork gently, slowly turning the bottle in one direction and the cork in another. The idea behind opening a bottle is to ease the cork out gently rather than cracking the bottle open with a loud pop and letting it foam. That may be a lot of fun, but it does nothing for the Champagne. When you pop off the cork, you allow the carbon dioxide to escape. That carbon dioxide is what gives Champagne its sparkle. If you open a bottle of Champagne in the way I've just described, then it can be opened hours before your guests arrive with no loss of carbon dioxide.

What do you do if you forget to chill the Champagne?

How many times have you realized you forgot to put the Champagne on ice and company is due any minute? What do you do?

Usually you put it in the freezer. Bad idea: *Don't* put Champagne in the freezer unless you tie a string around your finger to remind you the bottle's in there! The bottle can freeze and explode in a matter of fifteen minutes. Always chill Champagne in the warmest part of your refrigerator—the vegetable bin, for example. But if you're in a bind, and your guests are ringing the doorbell, and you realize the Champagne is not chilled yet, you have two options: (1) offer them a martini; (2) put the Champagne into an ice-filled bucket with water. It should be chilled and ready in 20 minutes.

Champagne Pet Peeves

After so many years in this business, I still can't figure out why so many people ruin perfectly good Champagne.

For instance, the Kir Royale, when the bartender adds crème de cassis (black-currant liquer) to Champagne. It cuts the acidity and adds sweetness to the wine, which is a shame, after the winemaker took so many years to get the wine to be dry.

The worst offender is the Mimosa, the Sunday brunch drink—Champagne and orange juice. I *love* people who only drink Dom Pérignon Mimosas. They're not going to taste anything. They may as well drink orange juice with club soda.

The other real offender is the Champagne Cocktail. The bartender adds bitters, orange peel, and sugar. Put it all together and then you add a great Champagne. What are you doing? Destroying the taste of Champagne.

Should I go on?

There's a time and place for everything. The examples described above are good occasions to buy an inexpensive sparkling wine at $4.99–$6.99 a bottle. If you use authentic Champagne for mixed drinks, you'll be wasting your money—unless, of course, you want to impress someone.

Which glasses should Champagne be served in?

No matter which Champagne you decide to serve, you should serve it in the proper glass. There's a little story behind the Champagne glass, dating back to Greek mythology. The first "coupe" was said to be moulded from the breast of Helen of Troy. The Greeks believed that wine-drinking was a sensual experience, and it was only fitting that the most beautiful woman take part in shaping the chalice.

Centuries later, Marie Antoinette, Queen of France, decided it was time to create a new Champagne glass. She had coupes moulded to her own breasts, which changed the shape of the glass entirely, since Marie Antoinette was—shall we say—a bit more endowed than Helen of Troy.

The glasses shown below are the ones commonly used today—the flute and the tulip-shaped glass. Champagne does not lose its bubbles as quickly in these glasses as it did in the old-fashioned model.

As beautiful as Helen was, the resulting glass was admittedly wide and shallow.

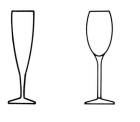

145

wine and food

Champagne is one of the most versatile wines that you can drink with a number of foods, from apéritif to dessert. Here are some Champagne-and-food combinations that a few experts suggest:

Christian Bizot (Bollinger)—Mr. Bizot's favorite accompaniments to Champagne are a cheese soufflé made with a mild cheese like Gruyère, or grilled fish with a light cream sauce, but not too spicy. He explains, "The heavier the food, the heavier the style of Champagne."

Another favorite of Mr. Bizot is Bollinger R.D. with game meats.

Some dishes that Mr. Bizot finds do *not* do justice to the wine: melon, because the sugary taste offsets the taste of the Champagne; vinegar, as in a salad dressing, or vinaigrette; any dessert with Brut Champagne.

Claude Taittinger (Taittinger)—First of all, Mr. Taittinger's general rule is: "Never with sweets." He prefers to serve Champagne with warm, cooked oysters, or as an apéritif with small hors d'oeuvres. He doesn't serve Champagne with cheese because, he says, "The bubbles do not go well." He prefers red wine with cheese.

Christian Pol Roger—With Brut non-vintage: light hors d'oeuvres, mousse of pike. With vintage: pheasant, lobster, other seafood. With rosé: a strawberry dessert.

What's the difference between Champagne and sparkling wine?

As I've already mentioned, Champagne is the wine that comes from the Champagne region of France. In my opinion, it is the best sparkling wine in the world, because the region has the ideal combination of elements conducive to excellent sparkling-wine making. The soil is fine chalk, the grapes are the best grown anywhere for sparkling wine, and the location is perfect. This combination of soil, climate, and grapes is reflected in the wine.

Sparkling wine, on the other hand, is produced in many areas, and the quality varies from wine to wine. The Spanish produce the popular Codorniu and Freixenet—both excellent values and good sparkling wines, known as *cavas*. The German version is called *Sekt*. Italy has *spumante,* which means "sparkling." The most popular Italian sparkling wine in the United States is Asti Spumante.

New York State and California are the two main producers of sparkling wine in this country. New York is known for Great Western, Taylor, and Gold Seal. California produces many fine sparkling wines, such as Domaine Chandon, Korbel, Piper-Sonoma, Schramsberg, Mumm Cuvée Napa, Roederer Estate, and Domaine Carneros. Many of the larger California wineries also market their own sparkling wines.

Domaine Chandon is owned by the Moët-Hennessy Group, which is responsible for the production of Dom Pérignon in France. In fact, the same winemaker is flown into California to make the blend for the Domaine Chandon.

Piper-Sonoma is a joint venture of Sonoma Vineyards and the Champagne house of Piper Heidsieck.

Is Schramsberg only for Republicans? I'm not sure, but the late President Richard Nixon took some Schramsberg with him on his first visit to China, as did former President Ronald Reagan when he visited China in 1984.

Is there a difference between the way Champagne and sparkling wines are made?

Sometimes. All authentic Champagnes and many fine sparkling wines are produced by the *Méthode Champenoise*, described earlier in this chapter, and which, as you can see, is laborious, intensive and very expensive. If you see a bottle of sparkling wine for $3.99, you can bet that the wine was not made by this process. The inexpensive sparkling wines are made by other methods. For example, in one method, the secondary fermentation takes place in large tanks. Sometimes these tanks are big enough to produce 100,000 bottles of sparkling wine.

Another fortified wine is Madeira. Although not as popular as it once was, Madeira wine was probably the first wine imported into America. It was favored by the colonists, including George Washington, and was served to toast the Declaration of Independence.

The neutral grape brandy, when added to the wine, raises the alcohol content to 15%–20%.

Two other famous fortified wines are Marsala (from Italy) and Vermouth (from Italy and France).

For you historians, Puerto de Santa Maria is where Christopher Columbus's ships were built and where all the arrangements were made with Queen Isabella for his journey of discovery.

SHERRY

The two greatest fortified wines in the world are Port and Sherry. These wines have much in common, although the end result is two very different styles.

What exactly is fortified wine?

Fortified wine is made when a neutral grape brandy is added to wine to raise the wine's alcohol content. What sets Port apart from Sherry is *when* the winemaker adds the neutral brandy. It's added to Port *during* fermentation. The extra alcohol kills that yeast and stops the fermentation, which is why Port is relatively sweet. For Sherry, on the other hand, the brandy is added *after* fermentation.

Where is Sherry made?

Sherry is produced in sunny southwestern Spain, in Andalusia. An area within three towns makes up the Sherry triangle. They are:

Jerez de la Frontera

Puerto de Santa Maria

Sanlúcar de Barrameda

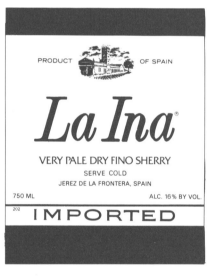

The Palomino grape accounts for 90% of the planted vineyards in Sherry.

Here's another abbreviation for you—PX. Do you remember BATF, TBA, QbA, AOC, and DOC? If you want to know Sherry, you may have to say "PX," which is the abbreviation for the Pedro Ximénez grape.

PX is used to make Cream Sherry, such as Harvey's Bristol Cream, among others. Cream Sherry is a blend of PX and Oloroso.

Which grapes are used to make Sherry?

There are two main varieties:

Palomino (this shouldn't be too difficult for horse lovers to remember)

Pedro Ximénez (named after Peter Siemons, who brought the grape from Germany to Sherry)

There are five basic types of Sherry:

Manzanilla—dry

Fino—dry

Amontillado—medium dry

Oloroso—dry or sweet

Cream—sweet

What are the unique processes that characterize Sherry production?

Controlled oxidation and fractional blending. Normally a winemaker guards against letting any air into the wine during the winemaking process. But that's exactly what *makes* Sherry—the air that oxidizes the wine. The winemaker places the wine in barrels and stores it in a bodega.

The Angel's Share

When Sherry is made, not only do winemakers let air into the barrels, but some wine evaporates as well. Each year they lose a minimum of 3% of their Sherry to the angels, which translates into 7,000 bottles per *day* lost through evaporation!

Why do you think the people of Sherry are so happy all the time? Besides the excellent sunshine they have, the people breathe in oxygen *and* Sherry.

So much for controlled oxidation. Now for fractional blending. Fractional blending is carried out through the *Solera System*.

What's a bodega?

No, I'm not talking about a Latino grocery store at 125th Street and Lexington Avenue in New York City. In Spain, a *bodega* is an above-ground structure used to store wine. Why do you think winemakers would want to store the wine above ground? For the air. Sherry is an oxidized wine. They fill the barrels approximately two-thirds full, instead of all the way, and they leave the bung (cork) loosely in the barrel to let the air in.

What's the Solera System?

The Solera System is an aging and maturing process that takes place through the dynamic and continuous blending of several vintages of Sherry that are stored in rows of barrels. At bottling time, wine is drawn out of these barrels—never more than one-third the content of the barrel—to make room for the new vintage. The purpose of this type of blending is to maintain the "house" style of the Sherry by using the "mother" wine as a base and refreshing it with a portion of the younger wines. Vintage Sherry just doesn't exist!

How do I buy Sherry?

Your best guide is the producer. It's the producer, after all, who buys the grapes and does the blending. Seven producers account for 60 percent of the export market:

1. González Byass
2. Croft
3. Pedro Domecq
4. Harvey's
5. Sandeman
6. Williams & Humbert
7. Savory and James

How long does a bottle of Sherry last once it's been opened?

Sherry will last longer than a regular table wine, because of its higher alcoholic content, which acts as a preservative. But once Sherry is opened, it *will* lose its freshness. To drink Sherry at its best, you should consume the bottle within two weeks of opening it, and keep the opened bottle refrigerated.

Of the Sherry consumed in Spain, 90% is Fino. As one winemaker said, "We ship the sweet and drink the dry."

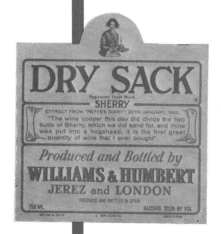

Wine and Food

Mauricio Gonzalez—He believes that one should always serve Fino well chilled. He enjoys having it as an apéritif with Spanish *tapas* (hors d'oeuvres), but he also likes to complement practically any fish meal with the wine. Some of his suggestions: clams, shellfish, lobster, prawns, langoustines, fish soup, or a light fish, such as salmon.

José Ignacio Domecq—He suggests that very old and rare Sherry should be served with cheese. Fino and Manzanilla can be served as an apéritif or with light grilled or fried fish, or even smoked salmon. "You get the taste of the smoke better than if you have it with a white wine," says Mr. Domecq.

Amontillado is not to be consumed like a Fino. It should be served with light cheese, *chorizo* (sausage), ham, or shish kebab. It is a perfect complement to turtle soup or a consommé.

Dry Oloroso is not commonly available in the United States, but according to Mr. Domecq, it is known as a sporty drink in Spain—something to drink before hunting, riding, or sailing on a chilly morning.

With Cream Sherry, Mr. Domecq recommends cookies, pastries, and cakes. Pedro Ximénez, however, is better as a topping for vanilla ice cream or as a dessert wine before coffee and brandy.

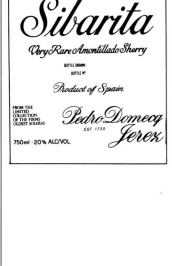

For further reading: *Sherry,* by Julian Jeffs.

PORT

Port comes from the Douro region in northern Portugal. In fact, in recent years, to avoid the misuse of the name "Port" in other countries, the true Port from Portugal has been renamed "Porto" (for the name of the port city from which it's shipped).

Just a reminder: Neutral grape brandy is added to Port *during* fermentation, which stops the fermentation and leaves behind up to 9–11 percent residual sugar. This is why Port is on the sweet side.

There are two types of Port:

Wood Port—This type includes Ruby Port, which is dark and fruity, blended from young non-vintage wines (Cost: $); and Tawny Port, which is lighter and more delicate, blended from many vintages, aged in casks—sometimes up to 40 years and longer (Cost: $$/$$$).

Vintage Port—This wine is aged two years in wood and will mature in the bottle over time (Cost: $$$$).

Port is a blend of more than six grapes.

Port wine has been shipped to England since the 1670s. During the 1800s, to help preserve the Port for the long trip, shippers fortified it with brandy, resulting in Port as we know it today.

Port is usually 20% alcohol. Sherry, by comparison, is usually around 18%.

As with Sherry, evaporation is a problem—some 15,000 bottles evaporate into the air every year.

Another less expensive method of making Tawny Port is to add white Port to a young Tawny Port. A true Tawny Port is always expensive. You get what you pay for.

FONSECA'S
Finest 1963
VINTAGE PORTO

Guimaraens - Vinhos S. A. R. L.

ESTABLISHED 1822

Bottled in Oporto   Product of Portugal

SOLE IMPORTERS FOR THE U. S. A.
SOVEREIGN IMPORTING COMPANY, INC.

ALCOHOL 21%
BY VOLUME

FARMINGDALE, NEW YORK
NY PERMIT NY-1-806

NET CONTENTS
750 ML

Is every year a vintage year for Port?

No, it varies from shipper to shipper. And in some years, no vintage Port is made at all. For example, in 1963 and 1970, two of the better vintages for Port, most producers declared a vintage. On the other hand, in 1962 and 1972, only four firms declared a vintage.

On average, only three years in ten are declared vintage years.

151

A "lodge" is the term used to describe a Port firm. Vila Nova de Gaia, a suburb of Oporto, is where Port's aging lodges are located.

In a typical year, 60% of the Port is Tawny and Ruby; 30% is vintage character; 7% is old Tawny; and 3% is vintage.

Quinta means individual vineyard.

A Port Primer:

LBV ("Late Bottled Vintage")— a wood Port made from a single vintage, bottled four to six years after the harvest. Similar in style to vintage Port, but lighter, ready to drink on release, no decanting needed.

"Colheita"—also from a single vintage, but wood-aged a minimum of 7 years.

Vintage Character—similar style to LBV, but a blend of vintages from the better years.

In France, the major importer of Port, the wine is used mainly as an apéritif.

Of the Port made in Portugal, 85–90% is for export.

The British are known to be Port lovers. Traditionally, upon the birth of a child, parents buy bottles of Port to put away for the baby until its 21st birthday; not only the age of maturity of a child, but also that of a fine Port.

How do I buy Port?

Once again, as with Sherry, the grape variety should not dictate your choice. Find the style and the blend that you prefer, but even more important, look for the most reliable producers. Of the Port available in the United States the most important producers are:

Cockburn
Croft
Dow
A. A. Ferreira
Fonseca
W. & J. Graham
Robertson's
Sandeman
Taylor Fladgate
Warre & Co.
Niepoort & Co., Ltd.
Quinta do Noval
Harvey's of Bristol
C. da Silva
Ramos Pinto

Best Bets for Vintages of Port

1963 1970 1977 1983 1985 1991 1992

Should vintage Port be decanted?

Yes, because you are likely to find sediment in the bottle. By making it a practice to decant vintage Port, you'll never be bothered by sediment.

How long will Port last once it's been opened?

Port has a tendency to last longer than ordinary table wine because of its higher alcohol content. But if you want to drink Port at its prime, drink the contents of the open bottle within one week.

matching wine and food

by Kevin Zraly and Andrea M. Immer

You've just tasted your way through eight chapters of this book and discovered at least a shopping-cart's worth of wines you really enjoy. And to what purpose? Food! The final stop on the wine odyssey—and the whole point of the trip—is the dinner table. Quite simply, wine and food were meant for each other. Just look at the dining habits of the world's best eaters (the French, the Italians, the Spanish); wine is the seasoning that livens up even everyday dishes. Salt and pepper shakers are a fixture of the American table, but in Europe it's the wine bottle.

Wine-and-Food Matching Basics

First, forget everything you've ever heard about wine-and-food pairing. There's only one rule when it comes to matching wine and food: the best wine to pair with your meal is whatever wine you like. No matter what.

Here's where I get to turn the tables on one of New York's most famous gossip columnists, whose wine order at Windows on the World was always, no matter the dish, Pouilly-Fuissé—on the rocks! If you know what you want, by all means have it. Worried that your preference of a light-bodied Liebfraumilch with a sirloin steak might not seem "right"? Remember, it's your own palate that you have to please.

What's wine-and-food synergy?

Sounds like a computer game for gourmets, right? If up until now you haven't been the wine-with-dinner type, you're in for a great adventure. Remember, the European tradition of wine with meals was not the result of a shortage of milk or iced tea. Rather, it results from what I call wine-and-food synergy—when the two are paired, both taste better.

How does it work? In the same way that combining certain foods improves their overall taste. For example, you squeeze fresh lemon onto your oysters, or grate parmesan cheese over spaghetti marinara, because it's the combination of flavors that makes the dish.

Now apply that idea to food-and-wine pairing; foods and wines have different flavors, textures, and aromas. Matching them can give you a new, more interesting flavor than you would get if you were washing down your dinner with, say, milk (unless you're dining on chocolate-chip cookies).

Do I have to be a wine expert to choose enjoyable wine-and-food matches?

Why not just use what you already know? Most of us have been tasting and testing the flavors, aromas, and textures of foods since before we got our first teeth, so we're all food experts! As I'll show you, just some basic information about wine and food styles is all you'll need to pick wines that can enhance your meals.

What role does texture play?

There is an obvious difference in texture or firmness between different foods. Wine also has texture and there are nuances of flavor in a wine that can make it just an adequate, or an unforgettable, selection with the meal. Very full-style wines have a mouth-filling texture and bold, rich flavors that make your palate sit up and take notice. But when it comes to food, these wines tend to overwhelm more delicate dishes (and to clash with boldy-flavored ones.) Remember, we're looking for harmony. A general rule is, the sturdier or fuller in flavor the food, the more full-bodied the wine should be.

Once you get to know the wines, matching them with food is no mystery. Here is a list with some suggestions based on the texture of the wine and the foods they can match.

White Wines

Light-bodied	Medium-bodied	Full-bodied
Alsace Pinot Blanc	Pouilly-Fumé	American
Alsace Riesling	Sancerre	Chardonnay★
Chablis	White Graves	Chablis Grand Cru
Muscadet	Chablis Premier Cru	Meursault
German Kabinett	Mâcon-Villages	Chassagne-
American Sauvignon Blanc★	St-Véran	Montrachet
Orvieto	Montagny	Puligny-
Soave	American Sauvignon Blanc★	Montrachet
Verdicchio	American Chardonnay★	
Frascati	Gavi	
Pinot Grigio		

Matching Foods

Light-bodied	Medium-bodied	Full-bodied
sole	snapper	salmon
flounder	bass	tuna
clams	shrimp	swordfish
oysters	scallops	lobster
	veal paillard	duck
		roast chicken

Red Wines

Light-bodied	Medium-bodied	Full-bodied
Bardolino	Cru Beaujolais	Barbaresco
Valpolicella	Côtes du Rhône	Barolo
Chianti	Burgundy premiers grands	Bordeaux great châteaus
Rioja-Crianza	crus★	Châteauneuf-du-Pape
Beaujolais	Bordeaux Petits	Hermitage
Beaujolais-Villages	Châteaux	American Cabernet
Burgundy village	American Cabernet	Sauvignon★
wines, premiers	Sauvignon★	American Merlot★
crus & grands crus★	American Merlot★	American Zinfandel★
	American Zinfandel★	
	Chianti Classico	
	Riserva	
	Dolcetto	
	Rioja Reserva and	
	Gran Reserva	

Matching Foods

Light bodied	Medium-bodied	Full-bodied
salmon	game birds	lamb chops
tuna	veal chops	leg of lamb
swordfish	pork chops	beefsteak (sirloin)
duck		game meats
roast chicken		

★Note that starred wines are listed more than once. That's because they can be vinified in a range of styles from light to full, depending on the producer. When buying these, if you don't know the style of a particular winery, it's a good idea to ask the server or wine merchant for help.

Do sauces play a major role when you're matching wine and food?

Yes, because the sauce can change the entire taste and texture of a dish. Is the sauce acidic? Heavy? Spicy? Subtly-flavored foods let the wine play the starring role. Dishes with bold, spicy ingredients can overpower the flavor nuances and complexity that distinguish a great wine.

Let's consider the effect sauces can have on a simple boneless breast of chicken. A very simply prepared chicken paillard might match well with a light-bodied white wine. If you add a rich cream sauce or a cheese sauce, then you might prefer a medium-bodied or even a full-bodied white wine. A red tomato-based sauce, such as a marinara, might call for a light-bodied red wine.

No-fault Wine Insurance

Drinking wine with your meals should add enjoyment, not stress; but it happens all too often. You briefly eye the wine list or scan the wine-shop shelf, thinking well, maybe . . . a beer. In the face of so many choices, you end up going with the familiar. But it can be easy to choose a wine to enjoy with your meal. From endless experimentation at home and in the restaurant, I've come up with a list of "user-friendly" wines that will go nicely with virtually any dish. What these wines have in common is that they are light- to medium-bodied, and they have ample fruit and acidity. The idea here is that you will get a harmonious balance of flavors from both the wine and the food, with neither overwhelming the other. Also, if you want the dish to play center stage, your best bets are wines from this list.

User-friendly Wines

Rosé wines
Virtually any rosé
or blush wine fills the bill

White wines
Pinot Grigio
American Sauvignon Blanc
German Riesling Kabinett and Spätlese
Pouilly-Fumé and Sancerre
Mâcon-Villages
Champagne and Sparkling Wines

Red Wines
Chianti Classico
Rioja Crianza
Beaujolais-Villages
Côtes du Rhône
Pinot Noir
Merlot

These wines work well for what I call "restaurant roulette"—where one diner orders fish, another orders meat, and so on. They can also match well with distinctively-spiced ethnic foods that might otherwise clash with a full-flavored wine. And, of course, all of these wines are enjoyable to drink on their own.

Wine and Cheese — Friends or Foes?

As in all matters of taste, the topic of wine and food comes with its share of controversy and debate. Where it's especially heated is on the subject of matching wine and cheese.

But wait! Isn't it common wisdom that wine and cheese are "naturals" for each other? It's absolutely true that a good cheese is sometimes the best food choice to make the most of a wine's flavors and complexity. That's why our wine-and-food dinners at Windows on the World always paired a cheese course with the last, best wine of the night (before dessert), usually a mature and full-bodied red, because this is the best way to showcase the wine.

The key to this match is in carefully selecting the cheese; therein lies the controversy. Some chefs and wine-and-food experts caution that some of the most popular cheeses for eating are the least appropriate for wine because they overpower it—a ripe cheese like Brie is a classic example.

The "keep-it-simple" approach applies again here. At Windows on the World, we found that the best cheeses for wine are the subtly flavored ones. Good bets: Parmigiano Reggiano, fresh Mozzarella, Pecorino, Talleggio, and Fontina from Italy; Chèvre, Montrachet, Tomme, and Gruyère from France; Dutch Gouda, English or domestic cheddar; domestic aged or fresh goat cheese and Monterey Jack.

My favorite wine-and-cheese matches:

Chèvre/fresh goat cheese— Sancerre, Sauvignon Blanc

Montrachet, aged (dry) Monterey Jack—Cabernet Sauvignon

Pecorino—Chianti Classico Riserva, Brunello

Parmigiano Reggiano—Amarone, Cabernet Sauvignon, Barolo

What to drink with Brie? Try Champagne or sparkling wine. And blue cheeses, because of their strong flavor, overpower most wines except—get ready for this—dessert wines! The classic (and truly delicious) matches are Roquefort cheese with French Sauternes, and Stilton cheese with Port.

Sweet Satisfaction:
Wine with Dessert, Wine as Dessert

I remember my first taste of a dessert wine—a Sauternes from France's Bordeaux region. It was magical! Then there are also Port, Madeira, Beerenauslese, to name a few—all very different wines with one thing in common: sweetness. Hence the name "dessert" wines—their sweetness closes your palate and makes you feel satisfied after a good meal. But with wines like these, dessert is just one part of the wine-and-food story.

"Wine with dessert?" you're thinking. At least in this country, coffee is more common, a glass of brandy or liqueur if you're splurging. But as more and more restaurants add dessert wines to their by-the-glass offerings, perhaps the popularity will grow for these kinds of wine. (Because they're so rich, a full bottle of dessert wine isn't practical unless several people are sharing it. For serving at home, dessert wines in half-bottles are a good alternative.)

At Windows on the World, we served the dessert wine a few minutes before the dessert itself, to prepare you for what was to come. But you certainly can serve a sweet dessert wine with the course. Here are some of the favorite wine-and-dessert combinations we served in The Cellar in the Sky:

Port—dark chocolate desserts, walnuts, poached pears, Stilton cheese

Madeira—milk chocolate, nut tarts, crème caramel, coffee- or mocha-flavored desserts

Pedro Ximénez Sherry—vanilla ice cream (with the wine poured over it), raisin-nut cakes, desserts containing figs or dried fruits

Beerenauslese and Late Harvest Riesling—fruit tarts, crème brulée, almond cookies

Sauternes—fruit tarts, poached fruits, crème brulée, caramel and hazelnut desserts, Roquefort cheese

Asti Spumante—fresh fruits, biscotti

Vouvray—fruit tarts, fresh fruits

Vin Santo—biscotti (for dipping in the wine)

Often, I prefer to serve the dessert wine as dessert. That way I can concentrate on savoring the complex and delicious flavors with a clear palate. It's especially convenient at home—all you have to do to serve your guests an exotic dessert is pull a cork! And if you're counting calories, a glass of dessert wine can give you the satisfying sweetness of dessert with a lot less bulk (and zero fat!).

WINE-buying STRATEGIES
for
YOUR WINE CELLAR

Buying and selecting wines for your cellar can be the most fun and interesting part of wine appreciation—besides drinking it, of course! You've done all of your studying and reading on the wines you like, and now you go out to your favorite wine store to banter with the owner or wine manager. You already have an idea of what you can spend (and haven't told your spouse!), and how many bottles you can safely store until they're paired with your favorite foods and friends.

Wine-buying has changed dramatically over the last 20 years. Many liquor stores have become wine-specialty stores, and the consumer and the retailer both are much more knowledgeable. Even 15 years ago, the wines of California, Australia and Chile were not the wines the consumer cared to buy. Back then the major players were the wines of France and Italy. Today there is so much more diversity in wine styles and wine prices, that it's almost impossible to keep up with every new wine and new vintage that comes on the market. You can subscribe, among many publications, to *The Wine Spectator, The Wine Enthusiast, Wine & Spirits,* or Robert Parker's, newsletter, *Wine Advocate* to help you with your choices, but ultimately you'll find the style of wine to suit your own personal taste.

In this book I don't recommend specific wines from specific years because I don't believe that everyone will enjoy the same wines, nor that everyone has the same taste buds as I do. I think it's very important that every year the consumer has a general overview of what's hot and what's not, and some strategies for buying wine.

There is, and will continue to be, an abundance of fine wine over the next few years. The vintage years of 1988, 1989, and 1990 in Bordeaux, Burgundy, Germany, and in Piedmont, Italy, will go down in history as the first time in decades that there have been three consecutive vintages of superior quality in these four areas. The 1990 to 1993 vintages for California Cabernet Sauvignon and Chardonnay are generally excellent. The 1991 vintage in Port, the first declared vintage since 1985, is now available. Although many of these wines are high-priced, there still remain hundreds of wines under $15 that you can drink now or cellar for the future.

Anyone can buy expensive wines! The real challenge is finding the best values, or the best wines at the best price. The following is a list of my buying strategy for my own wine cellar.

Everyday Wines ($10 and under)

California

Glen Ellen Proprietors Reserve

Robert Mondavi Woodbridge Selections

Trefethen Eshcol

Monterey Vineyards Classic

Napa Ridge

Louis Martini Cabernet Sauvignon

France

La Vieille Ferme Côtes du Ventoux

Michel Lynch

Maître d'Estournel

Côtes du Rhône Parallele "45" Jaboulet

Château Bonnet Blanc

Beaujolais-Villages Louis Jadot or Georges Duboeuf

Mâcon-Villages Caves de Vire Le Grand Cheneau

Spain

Marqués de Cáceres Rioja Crianza

Chile

Caliterra Cabernet Sauvignon

Santa Rita Cabernet Sauvignon

Los Vascos Cabernet Sauvignon

Cousino Macul Cabernet Sauvignon

Australia

Rosemount Chardonnay or Shiraz/Cabernet (Diamond Label)

Tyrrell's Long Flat White or Red

Lindemans Chardonnay Bin 65

Italy

Soave Classico, Anselmi

Montepulciano Red, Casal Thaulero

Washington State
Columbia Crest Merlot

Hogue Merlot

Sparkling Wines
Codorniu Brut Classico

Freixenet Brut

Once-a-Week Wines ($10 to $15)

France
Château Greysac

Château Larose Trintaudon

Château La Cardonne

Château Senejac

Crozes-Hermitage Domaine de Thalabert Jaboulet

Alsace Riesling Trimbach, Hugel or Zind-Humbrecht

Sancerre Archambault Clos de la Perrière

California
Sonoma-Cutrer Russian River Ranches

Ridge Zinfandel Paso Robles

Ferrari-Carano Fumé Blanc

Saintsbury Pinot Noir (Garnet)

Hawk Crest Chardonnay/Cabernet Sauvignon

Silverado Sauvignon Blanc

Kendall Jackson Chardonnay/Cabernet Sauvignon

Beaulieu Rutherford Cabernet Sauvignon

Fetzer Sundial Chardonnay

Meridian Chardonnay & Syrah

Benziger Merlot & Cabernet Sauvignon

Ridge Zinfandel, Sonoma

Buena Vista Sauvignon Blanc

Italy
Rosso di Montalcino Col d'Orcia

Chianti Classico Riserva Antinori & Badia a Coltibuono

Lungarotti Rubesco

Spain

C.U.N.E. Contino Reserva

Germany

Kabinett/Spätlese—for example Wehlener Sonnenuhr by J.J. Prum or
Niersteiner Olberg by R. Senfter

Sparkling Wines

Bouvet Brut

Korbel

Once-a-Month Wines ($15 and up)

California

Chardonnay

Mondavi

Chalone Gavilan

Ferrari-Carano

Sonoma-Cutrer Les Pierres

Cuvaison

Simi

Cabernet Sauvignon

Markham

Robert Mondavi

Sterling

Inglenook Cask

Clos du Val

Pinot Noir

Mondavi

Saintsbury Carneros

Acacia St. Clair

Calera

Zinfandel

Ridge Geyserville

Merlot

Markham

Clos du Bois

Duckhorn Napa Valley

FRANCE

La Doucette Pouilly Fumé

Château Carbonnieux Blanc

Château Olivier Blanc

Château Meyney

Château Gloria

Château Haut Batailley

Château Les Ormes de Pez

Château Prieuré-Lichine

Château Sociando-Mallet

Château Poujeaux

AUSTRALIA

Rosemount Show Reserve Chardonnay

Penfolds Bin 389

ITALY

Mastroberardino Taurasi

Antinori Chianti Classico Tenute Marchese Riserva

SPAIN

Pesquera Reserva

PORTS

Sandeman Founders Reserve

Fonesca Bin #27

ONCE-A-YEAR WINES ($$$$+)

It's easy to buy these kinds of wines when money is no object. Any wine retailer would be more than happy to help you spend your money.

CREATING AN EXEMPLARY RESTAURANT WINE LIST

Anyone who is even marginally aware of market trends knows that the popularity of wine has increased dramatically. Wine lists are no longer the province of an elite group of high-ticket, white-tablecloth culinary temples. There are ever-increasing ranks of customers who actively seek to enjoy wine in restaurants of all price levels.

To attract these potential customers, many a restaurateur has toyed with the idea of revamping and expanding his wine list. Yet, when confronted with the stark reality of such a task, many panic and accept the judgment of others, who have their own profit motives in mind. Once the restaurateur has acknowledged that it's time to start carrying more than house red, white, and rosé wines, he must lay the groundwork for building a list.

If you use the step-by-step method that follows, your wine list should complement your menu offerings, be attractively priced, offer an appealing selection, and be easy for the customer to select from and understand.

To illustrate: The hypothetical restaurant to which you've just taken the deed is a picturesque 100-seat establishment located in a moderate-size city. Your restaurant is open for both lunch and dinner, and doesn't possess any definite ethnic identity, falling under that umbrella label of "continental."

Here's a step-by-step procedure in question-and-answer format for building a wine list for your restaurant:

What's your competition?

Before you start to consider which châteaus to choose, or fret about whether to have 40 or 400 wines, take the time to investigate your market. Visit both the restaurants that attract the clientele you're aiming for (your target market) and the ones above and below your scale. Study how they merchandise wine, how well their staff serves it, and obtain a copy of their wine list—provided it's not chained to the sommelier's neck. Go during a busy dinner hour and observe how many bottles of wine are nestled in ice buckets or present on tables. Get a feeling for your competition's commitment to wine. See what's being done in your area, and what has yet to be done.

Can wine distributors offer help?

Contact the various suppliers in your area and explain to them what your objectives are. Ask them to suggest a hypothetical wine list—you're under no obligation to use it. Many wine distributors have specially trained people to work along with restaurateurs on their wine lists. They can also suggest ways of merchandising and promotion. Use them as a resource.

What's your storage capacity?

Wine requires specific storage conditions: temperature of 55°F (12.8°C), away from direct sunlight and excessive vibration. Your wine storage does not belong next to the dishwashing machine or the loading dock. How large a space do you have? Does it allow room for shelving? You'll want to store the bottles on their sides. How accessible is the wine to service personnel?

What are your consumers' preferences?

Preliminary research reveals that in the United States, 80 percent of the wine consumed is domestic, and 20 percent is imported. The consumer preferences of our target audience are predominantly for American and French wines.

How long should your list be?

This is, in part, determined by storage space and capital investment. For our hypothetical restaurant, we decided to feature 60 wines on the list. Initially, this might seem like a lot for a 100-seat restaurant, but consider that those wines will be divided between sparkling, red, white, and rosé, and encompass the regions of France, the United States, Italy, Spain, and Germany. Sixty is almost the minimum number which will allow you the flexibility to offer both a range of types and tastes and wine for special occasions, as well as for casual quaffing. We want our customers to know that wine matters in our restaurant.

What proportion of red to white?

In the present market, there's a decided consumer preference for white wines, and our wine list will reflect this. If our entrées were primarily red meats, we would ignore these figures and lean more heavily towards reds, because of their suitability to the menu offerings. However, our hypothetical restaurant has only three red-meat entrées out of ten, so the decision to feature more whites than reds is a sound one, based on both market trends and wine/food combinations.

How should prices be set?

Don't plan on paying your mortgage with profits from your wine list. Pricing is dictated according to your selections. Aim for 60 percent of these wines to be moderately priced. Why? Because this is the price category in which the highest volume of sales will take place. For our purposes, mid-priced wines sell for between $20 and $25. Therefore, we want 36 of our wines priced in this range. Of the remaining wines, 20 percent (12 wines) would be priced less than $20, and 20 percent for more than $25.

The percentage of profit realized on wine is less than that realized on cocktails. However, the dollar-value profit is greater since the total sale is much more. Too many restaurateurs have intimidated much of the potential wine market by stocking only very rare, expensive wines and pricing them into the stratosphere. You want a wine list that will enable all of your customers to enjoy a bottle (or two) of wine with their meal, without having to float a bank loan. The bulk of your customers are looking for a good wine at a fair price—not a rare vintage wine at $400 a bottle.

What's your capital investment?

Determine with your accountant the amount of money that you'll initially invest. Decide whether you want an inventory which will turn over in 30 to 60 days, or if you wish to make a long-term investment in cellaring wines. The majority of restaurants make short-term wine investments.

What will it actually cost?

Once we've decided on the number of wines on the list, and the general pricing structure, it's easy to determine what it will cost for one case of each wine. With some wines—the ones we anticipate will be very popular—our initial order will be for two cases, and for the more expensive wines, where sales may be sluggish, we'll start off with a half-case. Our 60-wine list will require an initial investment of approximately $6,000. Here's how we arrived at that "ballpark" figure:

Low-priced wines:
12 cases @ $60 per case $720.00

Medium-priced wines:
36 cases @ $108 per case $3,888.00

High-priced wines:
12 cases @ $144 per case   <u>$1,728.00</u>
                                     $6,336.00

Which categories of wine should be used?

Our wine list includes six sparkling wines (three French, two American, and one Spanish). There are 29 white wines, 24 red wines, and one blush, for a grand total of 60. Here is one example of how the categories might be broken down. Of course, each restaurant should choose the wines according to availability and price.

White wines (29)

FRENCH (10)

1 Mâcon Blanc

1 Chablis (Premier Cru)

1 Meursault

1 Puligny-Montrachet

1 Pouilly-Fuissé

1 Pouilly-Fumé or Sancerre

2 Alsace (1 Riesling,
    1 Gewurztraminer)

2 Bordeaux
    (1 Graves, 1 Sauternes)

AMERICAN (14)

1 Riesling

3 Sauvignon Blanc

10 Chardonnay

ITALIAN (2)

1 Soave

1 Pinot Grigio

GERMAN (2)

1 Rhein (Kabinett or
    Spätlese)

1 Mosel (Kabinett)

AUSTRALIAN (1)

1 Chardonnay

Red wines (24)

FRENCH (8)

1 Beaujolais

2 Burgundy (such as Nuits-St-Georges,
    Pommard, Volnay)

3 Bordeaux (different price categories)

2 Rhône Valley (1 Côtes du Rhône,
    1 Châteauneuf-du-Pape or
    Hermitage)

AMERICAN (11)

2 Merlot

2 Pinot Noir

1 Zinfandel

6 Cabernet Sauvignon

ITALIAN (3)

1 Chianti Classico Riserva

1 Bardolino or Valpolicella

1 Barolo or Barbaresco

SPANISH (1)

1 Rioja Reserva

AUSTRALIAN (1)

1 Shiraz or Cabernet Sauvignon

Blush (1)

1 White Zinfandel

Should I buy wine without tasting it?

Tasting the wines for the list is of utmost importance. If you've decided to feature a Meursault, contact your distributors and ask to taste all the Meursaults that conform to your criteria of availability and price. Tasting the wines blind will help you make selections on the basis of quality rather than label. These tastings represent quite an investment of time. To choose a wine list of 60 wines, you could easily taste three times that many.

Once you've narrowed the field, try pairing the wines with your menu offerings. If possible, include your staff in these tastings. The more familiar they are with the wines on the list and the foods they complement, the better they'll be able to sell your selections.

Recheck the availability of your selected wines. Place your orders. Remember, you don't have to buy 25 cases of each wine—you might initially purchase just six bottles of the more expensive wines.

What goes on the wine list?

There are many different styles of wine list. Some opt for long descriptions of the wine's characteristics and feature facts and maps of viticultural regions.

For our restaurant, we're going to adopt a very straightforward approach.

- The list is divided into categories by type, and each type is divided into regions.
- The progression is: sparkling wine, white, red, and blush.
- Our French wines will be broken down into regions—Alsace, Burgundy, Bordeaux, and so on. Each entry on the wine list will give the following information:
- Bin Number—This simplifies inventory and reordering, and assists both customer and staff with difficult pronunciation.
- Name of Wine—Be precise.
- Vintage—This is often omitted on wine lists by restaurateurs who want to be able to substitute whatever they can get. This practice is resented by anyone with a passing interest in wine. If the wine is non-vintage, the letters "NV" are used.
- Shipper—This information is very important for French wines, particularly those from Burgundy.

- The type, style, and color of the paper you choose for your wine list are personal decisions. However, double-check all spelling and prices before the list is sent to the printer. Your customers will be sure to point out any errors.

Your restaurant's open— what's next?

This is a guideline to establishing an initial list. At Windows on the World, with its high volume, we continually updated and revised the list to meet the requirements of our customers and the ever-changing wine market.

Once your list has been implemented, it's imperative that you track wine sales to determine how successful the list has been. Analyze your wine list with respect to the following factors:

- The number of bottles sold per customer (divide the number of bottles sold by the number of covers).
- How much white wine to red (by percentage)—you might find that you need more or fewer whites, more or fewer reds.
- The average price of a bottle of wine sold in the first three months.
- The ten most popular wines on the list.
- Instruct your staff to report any diner's request for a wine that's not on your list.

The steps involved in compiling our hypothetical list of 60 wines are the same steps that are used in compiling larger, more ambitious lists. Obviously, this list only highlights the major areas—60 wines barely scratch the surface of what's available. True, with this size restriction we're unable to give great depth of selection, but it's still a list where the average customer would find something appealing.

If you've taken the time to read this section, you now have a good idea of the task involved in creating a balanced wine list. For most restaurateurs, who have many other pressing concerns and responsibilities, the logistics of creating a wine list may seem Olympian. This checklist was offered to take some of the mystery out of this task.

WINE SERVICE IN RESTAURANTS — WHAT'S RITUAL AND WHAT'S REQUIRED

By Raymond Wellington

The wine market of the 1980s and 1990s has brought consumers a greater awareness of how wine is presented in American restaurants. Many people learn about wines by ordering them in restaurants, where they have the opportunity to sample and experiment, not only with wine, but with wine-and-food combinations. Decisions about how to stock a home cellar are frequently reached in this way. In restaurants noted for their wine lists, there is often the added pleasure of drinking a wine that's no longer available in retail stores.

Unfortunately, many restaurants have turned the simple task of ordering wine into a seemingly complex ritual involving sommeliers, tastevins, and intimidating lists that resemble telephone books. Add to that words such as "breathing" and "decanting," and you suddenly have a complicated situation on your hands.

Ordering wine should not be an intimidating ordeal. In fact, some restaurants make it relatively simple by providing straightforward wine lists and waiters or captains who have been properly trained to make sensible suggestions. Other restaurants make it more difficult, but whether you're in a grand, full-service restaurant or your favorite bistro, there are some basics to keep in mind.

The first problem you'll often encounter is actually obtaining the wine list. It's mystifying how difficult that can be sometimes. A restaurant genuinely interested in selling wine provides its wine list right along with the menu. If the wine list doesn't appear, or if you want to start the meal with wine before seeing a menu, then immediately ask for the list. With a little luck, they'll have more than one or two copies on hand!

The Wine List

Regardless of format, there is certain information that any good wine list should provide. First and foremost is the complete name of the wine. For example, if a wine list simply reads "Chambolle-Musigny," then the list is incomplete. It also means that the restaurant will make you work a little bit to find out exactly which wines are actually available. The complete name of the wine should be something like "Chambolle-Musigny, Domaine Groffier 1990." As you have learned by now, there could be many different producers of Chambolle-Musigny, and which producer could make a world of difference. The vintage is also essential: There's a vast difference between, say, a 1987 Chambolle-Musigny and one from 1990 (a superior vintage). If a wine is listed without a producer, or without a vintage, then ask the waiter. If the waiter doesn't know, let him or her find out and perhaps bring a bottle to show you.

The majority of American restaurants have neither wine stewards nor sommeliers (as they're sometimes called). In restaurants that are concerned with their wine selections and service, waiters and waitresses are often trained to be able to suggest wines. If a sommelier is available, however, it's usually worth taking advantage of his or her services.

The Sommelier

"Who is that person with the ashtray around his neck?" It's commonplace, if not downright fashionable, to deride the sommelier as someone who's condescending, pretentious, less knowledgeable than his guests, and sporting an odd costume adorned with keys, "ashtrays" on chains (the *tastevin*), and other seemingly mystical paraphernalia. This tarnished image of the sommelier has resulted, at least in part, from the practice of restaurateurs who have misunderstood the sommelier's position and who've appointed someone unqualified for the job. As restaurant patrons become better informed about wine, eatery owners are realizing the importance of having someone in the dining room who can knowledgeably discuss wine selections.

Often, when the services of a sommelier are available, the only way to avail yourself of such services is to ask. The sommelier need not be someone "to be reckoned with," but may be the one person who can help orchestrate and enliven your entire meal. Using a competent sommelier offers two advantages: He or she has tasted the wines on the list more recently than you, and he or she also knows how the menu items you ordered are actually being prepared.

Selecting a Wine

Whether you're ordering from a sommelier or from a waiter, there are a number of points to keep in mind. First, it's perfectly reasonable to keep the list and look it over for a few minutes before discussing your choices.

Second, if you want suggestions, give the sommelier or waiter something to work with. Do you have a particular wine region in mind? For example, if you've been dreaming about a fabulous California Chardonnay all week, say so!

Next, consider the style of wine you'd like. Do you or your guests want something light and direct, or do you prefer more aggressive, heavier wines? What price range are you thinking of? There's nothing wrong with saying you want something under $25. You can also do this by pointing to a price on the list and saying you want something "along these lines."

If wines are suggested that aren't on the list, the waiter or sommelier should tell you the price, along with the vintage, just as waiters and captains quote the prices of daily specials. If they don't tell you, then ask; no one wants to risk apoplexy when the check arrives!

When ordering more than one wine, discuss when the wines are to be served. The best rule of thumb is to have them all brought out—and even opened—as soon as you order them. This enables you to see that the correct wine is at the table, and you don't have to worry that the waiter will be otherwise engaged when you want your wine.

Opening the Wine

How often does it happen that after arriving at your selections, you wait and watch as the waiter fumbles with the cork—perhaps even breaking it—before successfully withdrawing it from the bottle? There's a right way and a wrong way to open a bottle of wine, or at least one method that works better than others.

Of the many different kinds of corkscrews and cork-pullers available, the most efficient and easiest tool to use is the pocket model of the "Screwpull," a patented device that includes a knife and a very long screw. Simply by turning in one continuous direction, the cork is extracted effortlessly. This is the best type of corkscrew for home use, and because it is gentle, it is best for removing long, fragile corks from older wines.

The corkscrew most commonly used in restaurants is the "waiter's corkscrew." Small and flat, it contains a knife, screw, and lever, all of which fold neatly into the handle.

When opening a wine bottle, the first step is to remove the capsule. You can accomplish this best by cutting around the neck on the underside of the bottle's lip. Once you remove the capsule, wipe the top of the cork clean—often dust or mould adheres to the cork while the wine is still at the winery, and before the capsule is put on the bottle. Next, insert the screw and turn it so that it goes as deeply as possible into the cork. Sometimes you'll need to raise the cork slightly and then turn the screw a bit further into it. This prevents breaking the cork.

The Tasting Ritual

Once you extract the cork, the "tasting ritual" begins. At this point the waiter should present the cork to the person who ordered the wine. Most people believe they're supposed to sniff the cork. This is really unnecessary, as it is the wine itself you want to smell. After all, a cork smells like a cork! The cork is presented so you can check its condition and authenticity. A moist cork is a good sign, a dry cork suggests there may have been a storage problem. If a cork is dried out, air may have gotten into the bottle and oxidized the wine. A dried-out cork could mean the wine has been stored upright rather than on its side.

Smelling and tasting are obviously the next two steps. At this point you are looking for flaws that render the wine unacceptable. When tasting wine, remember that anyone may be unsure after the first taste. Taste it again, take a moment and concentrate.

There are several valid reasons to reject a bottle of wine. For example, a bottle of wine might be "corky" or "maderized." It doesn't take extensive tasting experience to detect these flaws. Having the experience even once is usually enough to lock it in your taste memory. A "corky" bottle is one that smells strongly of mould: the result of a bad cork, not poor winemaking. A maderized wine has the distinct aroma of sweet Sherry or Madeira, hence the term. This is frequently the result of poor storage or exposure to heat.

A more experienced taster may detect excessive sulphur in the nose. This smell often dissipates with a bit of swirling; if it doesn't, it may make the wine unpleasant and worthy of rejection.

Policies regarding rejected wine vary among restaurants. Some restaurants will take a bottle back without question; others may take issue with a guest's complaint. It's extremely poor business for a restaurateur to put a customer on the spot and challenge his or her taste. If a very expensive wine, say over $50, is rejected, it's not uncommon for the restaurant owner or manager to come to the table and taste the wine.

Many places have no established policy, but handle each situation individually. At Windows on the World, incidentally, out of 10,000 bottles of wine sold in a month, only about a dozen were rejected.

WINE GLASSES

Whether you're dining out or you're at home, the enjoyment of food and wine is enhanced by fine silver, china, linen, and, of course, glassware. Wine glasses that are artfully etched, rose-tinted or perhaps green-stemmed may be lovely to look at and handle, but they're not really appropriate for the service of fine wine. The color of wine is as much a part of its pleasure and appeal as is its bouquet and flavor. Glasses which alter or obscure the color of wine detract from the wine itself. The most suitable wine glasses are those of clear glass with a bowl large enough to allow for swirling—that nervous habit which by now you have no doubt acquired!

The perfect size glass for a white or red wine is about ten ounces. To allow for swirling and the development of the wine's bouquet, a wine glass should not be filled more than halfway. Therefore, glasses that hold less than ten ounces are really too small.

A variety of shapes are available, and personal preferences should guide you when selecting glasses for home use. Some shapes, however, are better suited for certain wines than for others. For example, a glass which closes in a bit at the top helps to concentrate the bouquet of a white wine and also helps it keep its chill. Larger, balloon-shaped glasses are more appropriate for red wines.

There are three popular styles of Champagne glasses. The most common and least desirable is the saucer-shaped *coupe*. Awkward to balance, these glasses also tend to dissipate Champagne's bubbles. If you consider how much effort has gone into getting those bubbles in the Champagne in the first place, you'll understand why the *coupe* glass is so inappropriate!

The most suitable Champagne glasses and the ones more and more restaurants are using are the tulip or the Champagne flute. These narrow glasses hold between four and eight ounces, and they allow the bubbles to rise from a single point. The tulip shape also helps to concentrate the bouquet.

Port or Sherry is best served in smallish, narrow glasses with a straight chimney shape. Four to six ounces is the ideal size for this type.

The Decanting and Breathing Controversy

There is something romantic—if intimidating—conjured up by the image of a sommelier in black tie peering over a candle and solemnly pouring wine into a crystal decanter. There are good reasons for decanting a wine, although many restaurants go to an extreme: Either they decant many more wines than necessary, or they don't decant even those wines that require it. Where is the sensible ground in all of this, and what is the best way to decant a bottle of wine?

There are two primary reasons for decanting wine: (1) to separate the wine from the sediment and (2) to aerate the wine.

As far as aeration is concerned, no general rule applies to all red wines. Many theories have been put forth about the benefit to be derived from aerating, or letting a wine "breathe" before serving it. Our experience at Windows on the World suggested that the vast majority of red wines don't improve with "breathing." There's no question that some wines do, but these are the exceptions, and your own experience should serve as your guide. If you order a wine that you believe improves with a little bit of air, either have it decanted, or at least have the wine poured into glasses that you can swirl rather than simply removing the cork and letting the bottle stand. This last option is at once the most common practice in restaurants and the least effective. Think about it: By simply removing the cork, how much air is actually in contact with the wine?

How to Decant a Bottle of Wine

1. Completely remove the capsule from the neck of the bottle. This will enable you to see the wine clearly as it passes through the neck.

2. Light a candle. Most red wines are bottled in very dark green glass, making it difficult to see the wine pass through the neck of the bottle. A candle will give you the extra illumination you need. Anything else would do, but candles keep things simple.

3. Hold the decanter (a carafe or glass pitcher can also be used for this purpose) firmly in your hand.

4. Hold the wine bottle in your other hand, and gently pour the wine into the decanter while holding both over the candle at such an angle that you can see the wine pass through the neck of the bottle.

5. Continue pouring in one uninterrupted motion until you begin to see the first signs of sediment.

6. Stop decanting once you begin to see sediment.

AWARd-wiNNiNG wiNE Lists

The restaurants listed below were chosen by *The Wine Spectator*, the largest-selling wine newspaper in the United States, for having the best lists in the country.

Amelio's
San Francisco, California

The American Hotel
Sag Harbor, New York

The Angus Barn
Raleigh, North Carolina

Anthony's in the Catalinas
Tucson, Arizona

Anthony's Pier 4
Boston, Massachusetts

Aux Beaux Champs
Washington, D.C.

Bern's Steak House
Tampa, Florida

Beverly's
Coeur d'Alene, Idaho

Billy Crews Dining Room
Santa Teresa, New Mexico

Bluepoint Oyster Bar & Restaurant
Providence, Rhode Island

Brennan's Restaurant
New Orleans, Louisianna

Carlos Restaurant
Highland Park, Illinois

The Carnelian Room
San Francisco, California

Casanova Restaurant
Carmel, California

The Cellar
Fullerton, California

The Chanticleer Inn
Nantucket Island, Massachusetts

Charley's 517 Restaurant
Houston, Texas

Charlie Trotter's
Chicago, Illinois

The Chronicle
Pasadena, California

The Colony Restaurant
Longboat Key, Florida

Crabtree's Kittle House
Chappaqua, New York

Del Baffo
Menlo Park, California

The Dining Room
Chicago, Illinois

The Dining Room
Gleneden Beach, Oregon

The Down Under
Fort Lauderdale, Florida

El Paseo Restaurant
Mill Valley, California

Elario's Restaurant
La Jolla, California

Etienne's Different Points of View
Phoenix, Arizona

Felidia Ristorante
New York, New York

Five Crowns
Corona del Mar, California

Flagstaff House Restaurant
Boulder, Colorado

Florentine Dining Room
Palm Beach, Florida

The Forge
Miami Beach, Florida

Fournou's Ovens
San Francisco, California

The French Room
San Francisco, California

The Hermitage Inn
Wilmington, Vermont

The Inn at Sawmill Farm
West Dover, Vermont

Italian Village Restaurant
Chicago, Illinois

Jean-Louis at the Watergate Hotel
Washington, D.C.

Kingston 1686 House
Kingston, New Hampshire

La Petite Auberge
Cresskill, New Jersey

La Rive Gauche
Palos Verdes, California

Le Cirque
New York, New York

Le Français
Wheeling, Illinois

Le Moulin
Reno, Nevada

Lutèce
New York, New York

The Madison Park
Greensboro, North Carolina

The Manor
West Orange, New Jersey

Mr. Stox
Anaheim, California

Montrachet
New York, New York

Pacific's Edge Restaurant
Carmel, California

Park and Orchard Restaurant
East Rutherford, New Jersey

Patina
Los Angeles, California

Peppone
West Los Angeles, California

The Plumed Horse
Saratoga, California

The Ranch House Restaurant
Ojai, California

The Refectory
Columbus, Ohio

Rex il Restorante
Los Angeles, California

Rotisserie for Beef and Bird
Houston, Texas

The Sardine Factory
Monterey, California

Sierra Mar
Big Sur, California

Smith & Wollensky
New York, New York

Sparks Steak House
New York, New York

Starker's Restaurant
Kansas City, Missouri

Top o' the Cove
La Jolla, California

Valentino
Santa Monica, California

The Wild Boar
Nashville, Tennessee

The Wine Cask
Santa Barbara, California

Wine Merchant Restaurant
Akron, Ohio

The WineSellar & Brasserie
San Diego, California

Wooden Angel
Beaver, Pennsylvania

Glossary
and
pronunciation key

Acid: One of the four tastes of wine. It is sometimes described as sour or tart and can be found on the sides of the tongue and mouth.

Aligoté (Ahl-ee-go-TAY): A white grape grown in the Burgundy region of France.

Aloxe Corton (Ah-LOHSS Cor-TAWN): A village in the Côte d'Or in Burgundy, France.

Amarone (Ah-ma-ROH-nay): A type of Veronese wine made by a special process in which grapes are harvested late and allowed to "raisinate," thus producing a higher alcohol percentage in the wine and sometimes a sweet taste on the palate.

Amontillado (Ah-mone-tee-YAH-doe): A type of Sherry.

Anjou Rosé: A rosé wine from the Loire Valley in France.

A.O.C.: An abbreviation for Appellation d'Origine Contrôlée; the French government agency that controls wine production there.

A.P. number: The official testing number displayed on a German wine label that shows the wine was tasted and passed government quality-control standards.

Aroma: The smell of the grapes in a wine.

Auslese (OUSE-lay-zeh): A sweet white German wine made from selected bunches of late-picked grapes.

A.V.A.: An abbreviation for American Viticultural Area.

Barbaresco (Bar-bar-ESS-coh): A full-bodied, D.O.C.G. red wine from Piedmont, Italy; made from the Nebbiolo grape.

Barbera (Bar-BEAR-ah): A red grape grown primarily in Piedmont, Italy.

Barolo (Bar-OH-lo): A full-bodied D.O.C.G. red wine from Piedmont, Italy; made from the Nebbiolo grape.

B.A.T.F.: An abbreviation for Bureau of Alcohol, Tobacco, and Firearms; the government agency that controls wine production in the United States.

Beaujolais (Bo-zho-LAY): A light, fruity red Burgundy wine from the region of Beaujolais; in terms of quality, the basic Beaujolais.

Beaujolais Nouveau (Bo-zho-LAY New-VOH): The "new" Beaujolais that's produced and delivered to retailers in a matter of weeks after the harvest.

Beaujolais-Villages (Bo-zho-LAY vih-LAHZH): A Beaujolais wine that comes from a blend of grapes from designated villages in the region; it's a step up in quality from regular Beaujolais.

Beaune (Bone): French city located in the center of the Côte d'Or in Burgundy.

Beerenauslese (Bear-en-OUSE-lay-zeh): A full-bodied, sweet white German wine made from the rich, ripe grapes affected by "botrytis."

Blanc de Blancs (Blahnk duh BLAHNK): A white wine made from white grapes.

Blanc de Noir (Blahnk duh NWAHR): A white wine made from red grapes.

Botrytis cinerea (Bow-TRIED-iss Sin-eh-RAY-ah): A mould that forms on the grapes, known also as "noble rot," which is necessary to make Sauternes and the rich German wines Beerenauslese and Trockenbeerenauslese.

Bouquet: The smell of the wine.

Brix (Bricks): A scale that measures the sugar level of the unfermented grape juice (must).

Brunello di Montalcino (Brew-NELL-oh dee Mon-tahl-CHEE-no): A high-quality D.O.C.G. red Italian wine from the Tuscany region.

Brut (Brute): The driest style of Champagne.

Cabernet Franc (Cah-burr-NAY FRAHNK): A red grape of the Bordeaux region of France.

Cabernet Sauvignon (Cah-burr-NAY Sow-vee-NYOH): The most important red grape grown in the world, which yields many of the great wines of Bordeaux and California.

Chablis (Shah-BLEE): The northernmost region in Burgundy; a wine that comes from Chardonnay grapes grown anywhere in the Chablis district.

Chambolle-Musigny (Shahm-BOWL Moos-een-YEE): A village in the Côte d'Or in Burgundy, France.

Champagne: The region in France that produces the only sparkling wine to be authentically entitled Champagne.

Chaptalization: The addition of sugar to the must (fresh grape juice) before fermentation.

Chardonnay (Shahr-dun-NAY): The most important and expensive white grape, now grown all over the world; nearly all French white Burgundy wines are made from 100 percent Chardonnay.

Chassagne-Montrachet (Shahs-SAHN-ya MOWN-rah-SHAY): A village in the Côte d'Or in Burgundy, France.

Château (Shah-TOH): The French "legal" definition is a house attached to a vineyard having a specific number of acres with winemaking and storage facilities on the property.

Château wine: Usually the best quality Bordeaux wine.

Châteauneuf-du-Pape (Shah-toh-NUFF-dew-POP): A red wine from the southern Rhône Valley region of France; the name means "new castle of the Pope."

Chenin Blanc: A white grape grown in the Loire Valley region of France and in California.

Chianti (Key-AHN-tee): A DOCG red wine from the Tuscany region of Italy.

Chianti Classico (Key-AHN-tee CLASS-ee-ko): One step above Chianti in terms of quality, this wine is from an inner district of Chianti.

Chianti Classico Riserva (Key-AHN-tee CLASS-ee-ko Re-SER-va): The best quality level of Italian Chianti; it is aged for a minimum of three years.

Cinsault (San-SO): A red grape from France's Rhône Valley.

Classified châteaus: The châteaus in the Bordeaux region of France that are known to produce the best wine.

Concord: A red grape used to make some New York State wines.

Colheita (Coal-AY-ta): The term meaning "vintage" in Portuguese.

Cosecha (Coh-SAY-cha): The term meaning "harvest" in Spanish.

Côte de Beaune (Coat duh BONE): The southern portion of the Côte d'Or in Burgundy; known especially for fine white wines.

Côte de Nuits (Coat duh NWEE): The northern portion of the Côte d'Or in Burgundy; known especially for fine red wines.

Côte d'Or (Coat DOOR): The district in Burgundy that is known for some of the finest wines in the world.

Côte Rotie (Coat Row-TEE): A red wine from the northern Rhône Valley region of France.

Côtes-du-Rhône (Coat dew ROAN): The Rhône Valley region of France; also the regional wine from this district.

Cream Sherry: A type of Sherry made from a mixture of Pedro Ximénez and Oloroso.

Crianza (Cree-AHN-za): The most basic and least expensive quality level of Rioja wine.

Crozes-Hermitage (Crows Air-mee-TAHZH): A red wine from the northern Rhône Valley region of France.

Cru Beaujolais: The top grade of Beaujolais wine, coming from any one of ten designated villages in that region of France.

Cru Bourgeois: (Crew Bour-ZHWAH) A list of more than 400 châteaus in Bordeaux that have been recognized for their quality.

Decanting: The process of pouring wine from its bottle into a carafe to separate the sediment from the wine.

Dégorgement (Day-gorzh-MOWN): One step of the Méthode

Champenoise, used to expel the sediment from the bottle.

Demi-sec (Deh-mee SECK): A champagne containing a high level of residual sugar.

D.O.C.: An abbreviation for Denominazione di Origine Controllata; the Italian government agency that controls wine production there.

D.O.C.G.: An abbreviation for Denominazione di Origine Controllata e Garantita; the Italian government allows this marking to appear only on the finest wines. The "G" stands for "Guaranteed."

Dolcetto (Dohl-CHET-toh): A red wine from Piedmont, Italy, that is similar in style to a Beaujolais wine.

Dosage (Doh-SAHZH): A combination of wine and cane sugar that is used in making Champagne.

Edelfaule (EH-del-foy-luh): A German name for the mould that forms on the grapevines when the conditions permit it. (*See also* **Botrytis cinerea** and "**Noble Rot.**")

Erzeugerabfüllung (AIR-tzew-ger-AHB-fue-lung): A German word for an estate-bottled wine.

Estate-bottled: Wine that's made, produced, and bottled by the vineyard's owner.

Extra dry: Less dry than brut Champagne.

Fermentation: The process by which grape juice is made into wine.

Fino (FEE-noh): A type of Sherry.

First growth: The highest-quality Bordeaux château wine from the Classification of 1855.

Flor: A type of yeast that develops in some Sherry production.

Fortified wine: A wine such as Port and Sherry that has additional grape brandy that raises the alcohol content.

French Colombard: A white grape grown in California and used to make jug wines.

Gamay (Gah-MAY): A red grape used to make Beaujolais wine.

Gamay Beaujolais: A red grape grown in California.

Garnacha (Gar-NAH-cha): A red grape grown in Spain that is related to the Grenache grape of the Rhône Valley region of France.

Gevrey Chambertin (Zhehv-RAY Sham-burr-TAN): A village in the Côte d'Or in Burgundy, France.

Gewürztraminer (Ge-VERTZ-tra-MEE-ner): The "spicy" white grape grown in Alsace, California, and Germany.

Gran Reserva: A Spanish wine that's had extra aging.

Grand Cru (Grawn Crew): The highest classification for wines in Burgundy.

Graves (Grahv): A basic dry wine from the Bordeaux region of France.

Grenache (Greh-NAHSH): A red grape of the Rhône Valley region of France.

Hectare: A metric measure that equals 2.471 acres.

Hectolitre: A metric measure that equals 26.42 U.S. gallons.

Halbtrocken: The German term meaning "semi-dry."

Hermitage (Air-mee-TAHZH): A red wine from the northern Rhône Valley region of France.

Jerez de la Frontera (hair-ETH day la fron-TAIR-ah): One of the towns in Andalusia, Spain, where Sherry is produced.

Jug wine: A simple drinking wine.

Kabinett (Kah-bee-NETT): A light, semi-dry German wine.

Landwein: A German table wine; one step above Tafelwein.

Liebfraumilch (LEEB-frow-milch): An easy-to-drink white German wine; it means "milk of the Blessed Mother."

Liqueur de Tirage (Lee-KERR deh Teer-AHZH): In the Méthode Champenoise, a blend of sugar and yeast added to Champagne to begin the wine's second fermentation.

Lodge: The English term for a Port firm.

Long-vatted: A term for a wine fermented with the grape skins for a long period of time to acquire a rich red color.

Mâcon Blanc (Mac-CAW blahnk): The most basic white wine from the Mâconnais region of Burgundy, France.

Mâcon-Villages (Mac-CAW vee-LAHZH): A white wine from designated villages in the Mâconnais region of France; a step above the Mâcon Blanc quality.

Malvasia (Mahl-vah-SEE-ah): A white grape grown in Italy.

Manzanilla (Mahn-than-NEE-ya): A type of Sherry.

Margaux (Mar-GO): A district in the Bordeaux region in France.

Mechanical harvester: A machine used on flat vineyards. It shakes the vines to harvest the grapes.

Médoc (May-DOCK): A district in the Bordeaux region in France.

Merlot (Mehr-LOW): The red "softening" grape grown primarily in the Bordeaux region of France.

Méthode Champenoise (May-TUD Shahm-pen-WAHZ): The method by which Champagne is made.

Meursault (Mehr-SOH): A village in the Côte d'Or in Burgundy, France.

Microclimate: A term that refers to an area that has a climate within a climate. While one area may be generally warm, it may have a cooler "microclimate" or region.

Morey-St-Denis (Mor-RAY san duh-NEE): A village in the Côte d'Or in Burgundy, France.

Mosel-Saar-Ruwer (MO-z'l sahr ROO-ver): A region in Germany that produces a light-style white wine.

Mousseux (Moo-SUH): The term for all French sparkling wines that are not produced in Champagne.

Müller-Thurgau (MEW-lurr TURR-gow): A cross between the Riesling and the Silvaner grapes of Germany.

Muscadet (Moos-cah-DAY): A light, dry wine from the Loire Valley of France.

Muscat Beaumes-de-Venise (Mus-CAT bome deh ven-EASE): A sweet fortified wine from the Rhône Valley region of France.

Must: Grape juice.

Nebbiolo (Nehb-bee-OH-loh): A red grape grown in Piedmont, Italy, produces some of the finest Italian wine.

"Noble Rot": *See* Botrytis cinerea.

Non-vintage Champagne: Champagne made from a blend of vintages (more than one year's crop); it is more typical of the house style than vintage Champagne.

Nose: The term used to describe the bouquet and aroma of wine.

Nuits-St-Georges (Nwee san ZHORZH): A village in the Côte d'Or in Burgundy, France.

Official Classification of 1855: A classification drawn up by wine brokers of the best Médoc châteaus of that time.

Palomino: The primary grape used to make Sherry.

Pauillac (PAW-yak): A district in the Bordeaux region of France.

Pedro Ximénez (PAY-droh he-MAY-nays): A grape used to make Sherry.

Petite Sirah: A red grape grown primarily in California.

Petits Châteaus: Lesser-known châteaus in the Bordeaux region that produce good-quality wines for reasonable prices.

Phylloxera (Fill-LOCK-seh-rah): A root louse that kills grape vines.

Piedmont (PEED-mont): One of the most important wine districts in Italy.

Pinot Blanc: A white grape grown primarily in the Alsace region of France.

Pinot Meunier (PEE-noh muhn-YAY): A red grape grown primarily in the Champagne region of France.

Pinot Noir (PEE-noh NWAHR): A fragile red grape that is difficult to grow; nearly all red French Burgundy wines are made from 100 percent Pinot Noir.

Pomerol (Palm-muh-ROLL): A district in the Bordeaux region of France.

Pommard (Poh-MAR): A village in the Côte d'Or in Burgundy, France.

Pouilly-Fuissé (Pooh-yee fwee-SAY): The highest-quality white Mâconnais wine.

Pouilly-Fumé (Pooh-yee fooh-MAY): A dry white wine from the Loire Valley region of France.

Pouilly-Vinzelles (Pooh-yee van-ZELL): A dry white Mâconnais wine.

Premier Cru: A wine which has special characteristics that comes from a specific designated vineyard in Burgundy, France, or is blended from several such vineyards.

Prestige Champagne: The highest-quality Champagne.

Proprietary wine: A wine that's given a brand name like any other product and is marketed as such, i.e., Riunite, Mouton-Cadet.

Puligny-Montrachet (Pooh-lean-YEE mown-rah-SHAY): A village in the Côte d'Or in Burgundy, France.

PX: An abbreviation for the Pedro Ximénez grape from Sherry.

Qualitätswein (Kval-ee-TATES-vine): A German term meaning "quality wine."

Qualitätswein mit Pradikat (Kval-ee-TATS-vine mitt pray-dee-KAHT): The highest level of quality German wine.

Reserva/Riserva: A term that means a wine has extra aging; it is often found on Spanish, Portuguese, and Italian wine labels.

Reserve: A term sometimes found on American wine labels. Although it has no legal significance, it usually indicates a better-quality wine.

Residual sugar: An indication of how dry or sweet a wine is.

Rheingau (RHINE-gow): A region in Germany.

Rheinhessen (RHINE-hess-en): A region in Germany.

Rheinpfalz (RHINE-faults): A region in Germany. The official name has now been changed to Pfalz.

Ribera del Duero: A winegrowing region in Spain.

Riddling: One step of the Champagne-making process in which the bottles are turned gradually each day until they are almost upside down, with the sediment resting in the neck of the bottle.

Riesling: A white grape grown primarily in Alsace, Germany, and California.

Rioja (Ree-OH-ha): A wine region in Spain.

Ruby Port: A dark and sweet fortified wine blended from non-vintage wines.

Sancerre (Sahn-SEHR): A dry white wine from the Loire Valley region of France.

Sangiovese (San-jo-VAY-zay): A red grape grown primarily in Tuscany, Italy.

Sauternes (Sew-TURN): A sweet white wine from the Bordeaux region of France.

Sauvignon Blanc (SOH-veen-yown BLAHNK): A white grape grown primarily in the Loire Valley, Graves, and Sauternes regions of France, and in Washington State and California (where the wine is sometimes called Fumé Blanc).

Sekt: A German sparkling wine.

Sémillon (Say-mee-YAW): A white grape found primarily in the Graves and Sauternes regions of Bordeaux, France.

Short-vatted: A term for a wine fermented with the grape skins for only a short time.

Silvaner: A white grape grown in Germany and Alsace.

Solera system (So-LEHR-ah): A process used to systematically blend various vintages of Sherry.

Sommelier (So-mel-YAY): The French term for cellarmaster, or wine steward.

Spätlese (SHPATE-lay-zuh): A white German wine made from grapes picked later than the normal harvest.

Spumante: An Italian sparkling wine.

Stainless-steel tank: A container that (because of its capability for temperature control) is used to ferment and age some wines.

St-Émilion (Sahnt Ay-meel-YOHN): A district in the Bordeaux region of France.

St-Estèphe (Sahnt Ay-STEFF): A district in the Bordeaux region of France.

St-Julien (Sahnt Zhoo-lee-EHN): A district in the Bordeaux region of France.

St-Véran (Sahn Vay-RAHN): A white Mâconnais wine one step above Mâcon-Villages in quality.

Sulphur dioxide: A substance used in winemaking and grape growing as a preservative, an antioxidant, and also as a sterilizing agent.

Süss-Reserve: The unfermented grape juice added to German wine after fermentation to give the wine more sweetness.

Syrah (See-RAH): A red grape grown primarily in the Rhône Valley region of France.

Tafelwein: A German table wine.

Tannin: A natural compound that comes from the skins, stems, and pips of the grapes and also from the wood in which wine is aged.

Tavel: A rosé wine from the southern Rhône Valley region of France.

Tawny Port: A Port that is lighter, softer, and aged longer than Ruby Port.

T.B.A.: An abbreviation for the German wine Trockenbeerenauslese.

Tempranillo (Temp-rah-NEE-yoh): A red grape grown primarily in Spain.

Thompson seedless: A white grape grown in California and used to make jug wines.

Trebbiano (Treb-bee-AH-no): A white grape grown in Italy.

Trocken: The German term for "dry."

Trockenbeerenauslese (Troh-ken-bear-en-OUSE-lay-zuh): The richest and sweetest wine made in Germany from the most mature grapes.

Tuscany (TUSS-cah-nee): A region in Italy.

Varietal wine: A wine that is labelled with the predominant grape used to produce the wine, i.e., a wine made from Chardonnay grapes would be labelled "Chardonnay."

Veronese wines: The wines from Veneto, Italy: Valpolicella, Bardolino, Soave, and Amarone.

Village wine: A wine that comes from a particular village in Burgundy.

Vin de Pays (Van deh Pay-EE): A French classification one step below V.D.Q.S.

Vino Nobile di Montepulciano (VEE-noh NOH-bee-leh dee Mon-teh-pull-CHAH-noh): A D.O.C.G. red wine from the Tuscany region of Italy.

Vins de Table (Van deh TAH-bluh): Ordinary French table wine.

Vintage: The year the grapes are harvested.

Vitis labrusca: A native grape species in America.

Vitis vinifera (VEE-tiss Vih-NIFF-er-ah): A European grape species used to make European and California wine.

Viognier (Vee-own-YAY): A white grape from the Rhône Valley region of France.

Volnay (Vohl-NAY): A village in the Côte d'Or region of Burgundy, France.

Vosne Romanée (Vohn Roh-mah-NAY): A village in the Côte d'Or region of Burgundy, France.

Vougeot (Voo-ZHOH): A village in the Côte d'Or region of Burgundy, France.

Vouvray (Voo-VRAY): The white "chameleon" wine from the Loire Valley region of France; it can be dry, semi-sweet, or sweet.

Wood Port: Ruby and Tawny Port; they're ready to drink as soon as you buy them.

Zinfandel: A red grape grown in California.

index

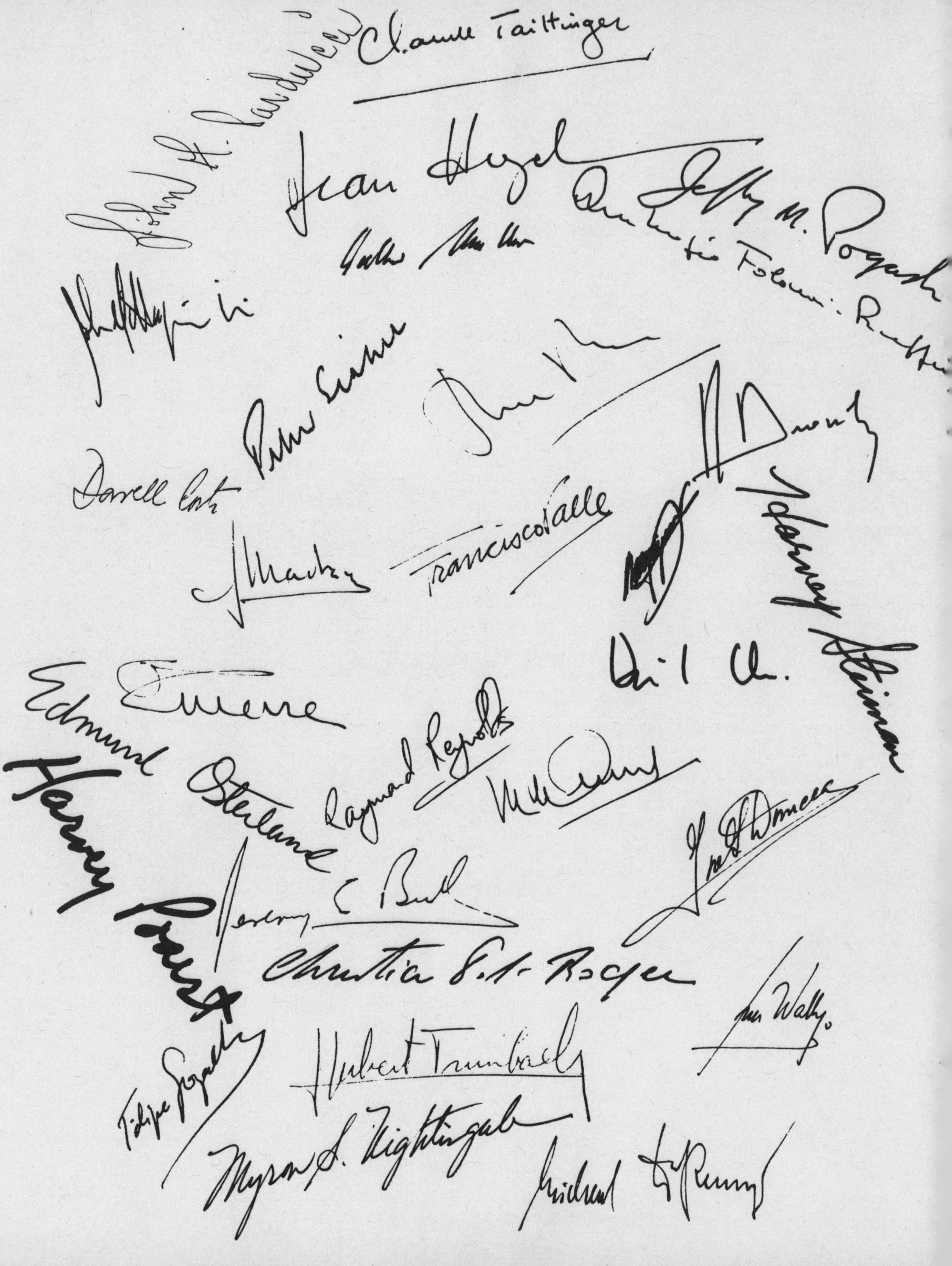
Claude Taittinger
Jean Hugel
Darrell Corti
Edmund Osterland
Hubert Trimbach
Myron S. Nightingale